New Approaches in Reasoning Research

Reasoning research has long been associated with paper and pencil tasks in which people's reasoning skills are judged against established normative conventions. However, there has been a recent revolution in the range of techniques, empirical methods and paradigms used to examine reasoning behaviour. *New Approaches in Reasoning Research* brings to the fore these new pioneering research methods and empirical findings.

Each chapter is written by a world-leading expert in the field and covers a variety of broad empirical techniques and new approaches to reasoning research. Maintaining a high level of integrity and rigour throughout, editors De Neys and Osman have allowed the experts included here the space to think big about the general issues concerning their work, to point out potential implications and speculate on further developments. Such freedom can only help to stimulate discussion and spark creative thinking.

The use of these new methods and paradigms is already generating a new understanding of how we reason; as such this book should appeal to researchers and students of cognitive psychology, social psychology and neuroscience, along with cognitive scientists and anyone interested in the latest developments in reasoning, rationality, bias and thinking.

Wim De Neys earned his Ph.D. in Cognitive Psychology from the University of Leuven, Belgium, in May 2003. Before being recruited as a tenured CNRS research scientist in France he worked as a post-doc at the University of California Santa Barbara, York University Toronto, Canada and the University of Leuven, Belgium. He is currently serving as Associate Editor for *Psychonomic Bulletin & Review* and Consulting Editor for the journals *Memory & Cognition* and *Thinking & Reasoning*.

Magda Osman earned her Ph.D. in Psychology from Brunel University, London, in 2001. She spent six years as a research fellow at University College London, where she continues to be an honorary research fellow. She now has a senior lectureship position at Queen Mary University of London. She is serving as Associate Editor for *Experimental Psychology* and consults on several national and international research council panels.

Current Issues in Thinking and Reasoning

Series Editor: Linden Ball

Current Issues in Thinking and Reasoning is a series of edited books which will reflect the state of the art in areas of current and emerging interest in the psychological study of thinking processes.

Each volume will be tightly focussed on a particular topic and will consist of from seven to ten chapters contributed by international experts. The editors of individual volumes will be leading figures in their areas and will provide an introductory overview.

Example topics include thinking and working memory, visual imagery in problem solving, evolutionary approaches to thinking, cognitive processes in planning, creative thinking, decision-making processes, pathologies of thinking, individual differences, neuropsychological approaches and applications of thinking research.

Emotion and Reasoning
Edited by Isabelle Blanchette

New Approaches in Reasoning Research

Edited by
Wim De Neys and Magda Osman

First published 2014
by Psychology Press
27 Church Road, Hove, East Sussex BN3 2FA

and by Psychology Press
711 Third Avenue, New York, NY 10017

Psychology Press is an imprint of the Taylor & Francis Group, an informa business

British Library Cataloguing in Publication Data
A catalogue record for this book is available from the British Library

Library of Congress Cataloging in Publication Data
New approaches in reasoning research / edited by Wim De Neys & Magda Osman.
pages cm.—(Current issues in thinking and reasoning)
Includes bibliographical references and index.
1. Reasoning (Psychology) 2. Decision making. 3. Cognitive psychology.
I. De Neys, Wim editor of compilation. II. Osman, Magda editor of compilation.
BF442.N49 2014
153.4'3—dc23
2013023804

ISBN: 978–1–84872–155–5 (hbk)
ISBN: 978–1–84872–156–2 (pbk)
ISBN: 978–1–31587–985–7 (ebk)

Typeset in Times New Roman
by Swales & Willis Ltd, Exeter, Devon

Contents

Contributors

Maria Augustinova
Laboratoire de Psychologie Sociale et Cognitive
LAPSCO (CNRS unit 6024)
Clermont University
34, av. Carnot
63037 Clermont-Ferrand Cedex
France

Linden J. Ball
School of Psychology
University of Central Lancashire
Darwin Building
Preston
Lancashire
PR1 2HE
UK

Jean-François Bonnefon
CLLE (CNRS Unit 5263)
University of Toulouse
Maison de la Recherche
5, allée A. Machado
31058 Toulouse Cedex 9
France

Grégoire Borst
LAPSYDE (CNRS Unit 3521)
Paris Descartes University, Sorbonne Paris Cité, University of Caen
46, rue Saint-Jacques
75005 Paris
France

Wim De Neys
LAPSYDE (CNRS Unit 3521)
Paris Descartes University, Sorbonne Paris Cité, University of Caen
46, rue Saint-Jacques
75005 Paris
France

Vittorio Girotto
Laboratory of Experimental Economics
University IUAV of Venice
Convento delle Terese, DD 2206
30123 Venice
Italy

Olivier Houdé
LAPSYDE (CNRS Unit 3521)
Paris Descartes University, Sorbonne Paris Cité, University of Caen
Institut Universitaire de France (IUF)
46, rue Saint-Jacques
75005 Paris
France

Sylvain Moutier
LAPSYDE (CNRS Unit 3521)
Paris Descartes University, Sorbonne Paris Cité, University of Caen
46, rue Saint-Jacques
75005 Paris
France

Magda Osman
Department of Psychology
School of Biological and Chemical Sciences
Queen Mary University of London
Mile End
London
E1 4NS
UK

Melanie Stollstorff
Institute of Cognitive Science
Psychology and Neuroscience Department
University of Colorado Boulder
Muenzinger D244
345 UCB
Boulder, CO 80309-0345
USA

Bastien Trémolière
CLLE (CNRS Unit 5263)
University of Toulouse
Maison de la Recherche
5, allée A. Machado
31058 Toulouse Cedex 9
France

1 New approaches in reasoning research

An introduction

Wim De Neys

Background

As a graduate student who started working in the reasoning field, one of the most frustrating obligations was to present my research to colleagues at the University of Leuven's Experimental Psychology Lab. The lab was huge (the equivalent to a small department in many other universities) and comprised of a large number of research groups that were working on a range of topics from visual perception, to memory and numerical cognition, to reasoning research. Once a year all lab members were expected to present their work to the whole group. These talks were typically quite interesting with a large turnout. They would also usually lead to engaging and stimulating discussions. I write typically and usually because this did not apply to talks by people in the reasoning group. Although our group was internationally renowned in the reasoning community, this was not reflected in the attendance at our talks. Water-cooler conversations[1] taught me that one of the reasons why people were reluctant to show up to talks on reasoning was because they felt it was an insular field of research, perceived at operating in isolation of advances in other fields. Quite a few colleagues also argued that reasoning research was limited in generating innovative methodologies and had really not moved beyond simple paper-and-pencil studies.

When I started attending major international conferences things didn't really improve there either. I was quite struck to discover that reasoning posters and talks tended to attract a very limited and select crowd. Discussions at opening receptions and conference dinners indicated that a lot of scholars in the international cognitive science community shared the views of my Belgian colleagues. In sum, in my experience there seemed to be a quite negative sentiment in the larger cognitive science community towards reasoning research in the late 90s.

Although I could see that there might have been some ground for this negative caricature in past work on reasoning, I also felt that it didn't apply to the work of the many young scholars in the reasoning field that I was getting to know. Indeed, contrary to what the wider community seemed to believe, I was seeing a wide range of new innovative approaches and interdisciplinary research efforts emerging. Although these new trends might not have made it to the mainstream reasoning journals or textbooks yet, the building blocks were definitely there.

At one of those early international conferences that I attended, I was fortunate enough to bump into Magda Osman. Over the years we have spent quite some time discussing the misperception about contemporary reasoning research and the need to showcase the newest approaches both inside and outside the field. Some time ago we decided we probably needed to stop whining and should try to do something about it. The result is the present book.

In a nutshell, our edited volume is designed to bring to the fore trends in research methods and research questions in contemporary reasoning research. As well as re-addressing misperceptions about reasoning research we also hope that the book will stimulate discussion within the reasoning field. Indeed, in addition to informing the wider scientific community about innovative new approaches in the reasoning field, this book should also help to reinvigorate the reasoning field by showing that the use of new methods and paradigms are generating new insights. In the end, we hope that the book will inspire new interest in young researchers inside and outside the reasoning field and boost attention for the study of what has been labeled the essence of our being: reasoning.

Book structure

Each chapter in the book is written by a leading expert and introduces one specific new approach or method. Content-wise our remit for the contributors was twofold:

1 We asked contributors to present their paradigm and briefly review their work for a general audience. The idea here was to arrive at a sort of comprehensive primer that would familiarize the non-expert reader with the approach and methodology.
2 We also wanted to allow authors more freedom than they would typically be given to make bold claims and speculate about the implication of their work. We still aimed to maintain a high level of integrity and rigor in the quality of work from our contributors but we also wanted to give the experts the space to think big about the general issues concerning their work. Bluntly put, we wanted them to have a chance to "speak freely": even if their research program was still new, we asked them to point out the potential bigger implications and further developments. We felt that such freedom would help to stimulate discussion and spark creative thinking.

Brief chapter overview

I present a very brief overview of the different contributions here. In the final chapter my co-editor, Magda Osman, presents a more in-depth discussion of the chapters and identifies common themes that connect the different approaches.

Chapter 2: Genes of rationality: building blocks for the neurobiology of reasoning (Melanie Stollstorff, University of Colorado Boulder)

Decades of reasoning research have shown that human reasoning is easily biased by erroneous intuitions or so-called heuristics. The work of Melanie Stollstorff concerns a highly contentious issue: the possible genetic basis of individual differences in heuristic bias susceptibility. In her chapter Stollstorff familiarizes the reasoning community with the genetic labeling method and reviews her fascinating findings.

Chapter 3: The rationality of mortals: thoughts of death disrupt analytic processing (Bastien Trémolière and Jean-François Bonnefon, University of Toulouse)

The human species enjoys uniquely developed capacities for analytic reasoning and rational decision-making, but these capacities come with a price: they make us aware of our inevitable physical death. Drawing on terror-management theory and dual-process theories of cognition, Trémolière and Bonnefon discuss the debilitating impact of mortality awareness on analytic reasoning. When made aware of their own death, reasoners allocate their executive resources to the suppression of this disturbing thought, therefore impairing their analytic thinking. Trémolière and Bonnefon discuss a wide range of intriguing consequences for all aspects of rational thinking that draw on executive resources.

Chapter 4: Negative priming in logicomathematical reasoning: the cost of blocking your intuition (Grégoire Borst, Sylvain Moutier and Olivier Houdé, Paris Descartes University and the University of Caen)

Many reasoning theories assume that sound reasoning requires the inhibition of heuristic intuitions that conflict with logical norms. Despite the popularity of this claim, direct memory-based evidence for the postulation of a belief inhibition process is often missing. In their chapter, Grégoire Borst, Sylvain Moutier and Olivier Houdé document how a classic negative priming procedure can be used in reasoning studies to validate the inhibition claim. Their findings show that one ironic consequence of belief inhibition is that previously inhibited intuitive knowledge can remain inaccessible on subsequent trials where the intuitive response could be helpful. The authors discuss the implications of their work for the debate on the nature of heuristic bias.

Chapter 5: Eye-tracking and reasoning: what your eyes tell about your inferences (Linden J. Ball, University of Central Lancashire)

How do our beliefs influence the way we reason? According to Linden J. Ball, one way of investigating this is to examine where people attend and how long they attend to certain information when presented with reasoning tasks. Linden J. Ball and his colleagues pioneered this line of work by using eye trackers. In this chapter, Ball introduces the eye-tracking methodology and illustrates how eye-tracking data can illuminate theories of reasoning. He also considers ways in which the eye-tracking methodology might be deployed in future studies to address questions regarding the optimal explanation of the biases that pervade people's reasoning.

Chapter 6: Self-perception and reasoning: how perceiving yourself as rational makes you less biased (Maria Augustinova, Clermont University)

Social psychologists have shown that the motivation to possess a desired characteristic results in self-perceptions that can have a strong impact on people's behavior. For example, when participants are led to believe that successfully completing a randomly selected task (e.g., solving a puzzle) is characteristic of high self-esteem and leadership potential, they will be more likely to complete it. The innovation by Maria Augustinova and her research team has been to take a paradigm that has been used to explore this behavior in the social cognition domain and apply it to the reasoning field. Her studies show that very basic self-perception manipulations can result in a dramatic decrease in biased responses on classic reasoning tasks. In her chapter Augustinova introduces this work and sketches implications for the reasoning community.

Chapter 7: Probabilistic reasoning: rational expectations in young children and infants (Vittorio Girotto, University IUAV of Venice)

The pioneering work of Vittorio Girotto and his colleagues focuses on the probabilistic reasoning skills of young children and preverbal babies. In his chapter Girotto introduces his approach and reviews his core findings. He clarifies how this work leads to the bold claim that all human beings possess a correct intuition of probability, regardless of their education and background.

Chapter 8: Reasoning research: where was it going? Where is it now? Where will it be going? (Magda Osman, Queen Mary University of London)

In the final chapter Magda Osman starts by putting things in a historical perspective. She considers the origins of reasoning research and the major traditional research themes and issues that emerged. From this, she discusses the new approaches that are presented in this book and tries to identify common themes that connect the different research strands. Against this background she also speculates about the future of reasoning research.

Note

1 This being Belgium, the phrase "conversations-in-a-local-bar-after-a-couple-of-beers" would have probably been more accurate.

2 Genes of rationality

Building blocks for the neurobiology of reasoning

Melanie Stollstorff

Introduction

Genes are the building blocks for life; from infancy to senescence, our genes play a role in making us who we are. Our genetics interact with the environment to make us unique individuals, capable of creative and novel ideas, and at times, "creative logic". Do our genes predispose us to logical errors? Here I will present some initial evidence that they do. These initial studies might be thought of as the building blocks for the study of reasoning from a neurobiological/genetic perspective.

Generally speaking, healthy adults can reason logically, but tend to make errors in predictable ways (i.e., heuristic biases). Upon learning about human reasoning biases, I'm sure that many individuals think to themselves, "not me!" and can readily provide examples of others whose logic is considerably more error-prone. One classic example of a reasoning heuristic is the belief-bias effect, which is a tendency to solve a reasoning problem based on one's beliefs or prior semantic knowledge rather than logical structure (Evans et al., 1983); that is, to be swayed by beliefs rather than logic. It is known that certain external factors, such as time pressure (Tsujii and Watanabe, 2010) and emotional content (Blanchette and Richards, 2004), increase reasoning bias. Are some people more sensitive to these factors and therefore more prone to logical errors than others? Yes! Internal factors, that is, those arising from within the individual such as working memory and inhibitory control, can influence reasoning bias (Handley et al., 2004). Various cognitive neuroscience methods have begun to shed light on the neurobiology of reasoning over the last 15 years including many types of neuroimaging studies (Goel, 2007; Goel et al., 2000; Luo et al., 2008; Prado et al., 2011; Tsujii and Watanabe, 2009). In this chapter, I will describe findings from a new field of reasoning research: reasoning genetics. Recent research has identified genes to be another internal source of variance that influences deductive reasoning and more specifically, belief bias (Stollstorff et al., 2012). It seems that our genetic make-up influences our ability to reason logically and can account for significant variance in errors which was previously unexplained. This chapter will highlight evidence that reasoning ability is, in part, determined by our genes.

While there is considerable research on cognitive biases in reasoning and some research on the effect of emotion on reasoning (Blanchette and Richards, 2004), little is known about how individual differences in emotional reactivity might enhance or diminish cognitive biases to influence the deductive reasoning process. I will describe a series of studies that investigate the effect of emotional content on bias in logical reasoning and how this behavior and its brain bases are modulated by a polymorphism for the serotonin transporter genotype (SERT) that is known to influence emotional reactivity. I will also explore how dopamine, known to influence cognitive control processes such as working memory and inhibition, can influence the neural bases of biased decision-making. I will conclude by briefly describing other neurobiological factors (neurotransmitters and genes that regulate them) that could help elucidate questions in the field of human reasoning.

Genes, brains and neurotransmitters

Our genetic code programs the building blocks for human thought. The essential neurobiological ingredients for reasoning, such as neurotransmitters, neurons and synapses, arise from our genes. Genes interact with the environment to produce individual differences in many aspects of human thought, feeling and behavior. These differences result, at least in part, from genetic polymorphisms. A genetic polymorphism arises from a mutation that occurred at some point in our evolutionary history that has been preserved and passed on through generations, especially if they promote survival. I will focus primarily on one common genetic polymorphism (the serotonin transporter gene: 5-HTTLPR or "SERT") and its effect on belief bias in emotional reasoning.

What do genes have to do with reasoning? Genetics provide a natural model to investigate individual differences in reasoning ability without having to manipulate anything experimentally. In animal models, scientists can have more flexibility; for example, they can inject dopamine into the basal ganglia and test the animal's behavior. However, human experimental manipulation of neurotransmitters is not as straightforward or scientifically controlled; we can administer drugs to patients with pre-existing conditions and occasionally even to healthy individuals. However, with genetics, we have a ready-to-go model: genetic polymorphisms exist among healthy humans that have known functional consequences on neurotransmitter function, sometimes localized to specific brain regions. It is a great experimental model and a wonderful tool to test psychological theory.

Genetics 101: the basics and the methods

The human genome is incredibly complex and molecular geneticists practically have their own language. However, the good news is that for our purposes, genetics can be quite simple to understand and to utilize in psychological research studies. Let me walk you through the process to clarify the methods and introduce some important basic genetic concepts: first, we ask participants to "spit in a cup". They provide a saliva sample into a specially prepared (or purchased) collection kit. Other common methods include collecting buccal cheek cells from the inside of the mouth or from blood draws. The end result, regardless of method, is a sample containing the DNA of the participant. Once the DNA is extracted from the saliva (or cheek cells or blood), they are genotyped for the specific polymorphisms of interest (or several of them).[1]

A polymorphism is a region in our genetic code that differs across individuals. A "functional" polymorphism is a part of our DNA strand with multiple forms that results in differential expression of the protein that it codes for, ultimately resulting in some type of individual difference in our biology, such as eye color. Typically, you might be interested in a single nucleotide polymorphism (SNP), which is a point in the strand of our DNA where one of those nucleotide pairs has been switched (e.g., from A to G). Popular/infamous examples of SNPs include: COMT (val-allele linked to schizophrenia (Egan et al., 2001)), or FTO (A-allele linked to obesity (Frayling et al., 2007)). Or you might be interested in a variable-number tandem repeat (VNTR) polymorphism, where a section or small chunk of the DNA strand is repeated a different number of times. Well-known examples of VNTRs include: APOE (E4-allele linked to Alzheimer's disease), DAT1 and DRD4 (10/10 DAT1 genotype and 7-repeat DRD4 alleles linked to ADHD (Cook et al., 1995; Rowe et al., 1998)), SERT (short allele linked to mood disorders (Caspi et al., 2003)).

Polymorphisms vary in their contribution to a particular behavior or disease. Some genes directly cause a disease; for example, if you inherit even one of the risk alleles (36-repeat allele or higher), you *will* develop Huntington's disease. Individuals who inherit the non-risk allele (<36 repeats) will not inherit this disease (Walker, 2007). For other genes, for example, BRCA1, you are at a much higher risk for breast cancer (50–80 per cent more likely to develop breast cancer) if you carry the mutation (Domchek et al., 2010) and therefore other contributing factors (genetic and/or environmental) must be involved as well. And yet for others, inheriting the risk alleles increases your risk only slightly (for example, ~4 per cent for the DAT1 10/10 genotype and ADHD (Waldman et al., 1998)). That leaves huge room for other genes and known or yet-unknown environmental factors to contribute, either by additive or interactive effects. To some critics, these low gene-to-behavior effect sizes render single polymorphism genetic studies useless. The contribution of a single polymorphism to a psychiatric disorder can be low and replication studies sometimes fail. However, I believe this is true of all aspects of biological psychology. It is difficult to predict with scientific precision any phenomenon that is itself somewhat vague. Many psychiatric disorders have no reliable biomarkers or tests and diagnosis is arguably subjective, based on manuals with different criteria depending on which continent the clinician is from. Genetics in psychology and cognitive neuroscience is in its infancy. But this is why, in my opinion, it is that much more important to focus our research efforts on genetics to begin to untangle this complicated puzzle of genes and behavior. Once a polymorphism is identified as a possible contributor to psychological function or dysfunction, we can, and should, begin to elucidate the mechanism by which this gene has its effect through psychological and cognitive neuroscience methods. Ultimately, these genetic polymorphisms influence the neurotransmitters that fuel the brain, which in turn gives rise to reasoning and errors in logic.

While genetic differences amongst us are complicated and surely interact with the environment as we develop, we are beginning to elucidate the mechanisms that underlie human reasoning and natural tendencies towards specific heuristics and biases. Humans differ in their reaction to environmental triggers that lead to irrational decisions. The large body of reasoning literature in psychology describes the nature of these patterns in errors and has even begun to elucidate the cognitive bases for these irrational biases. Here, we begin to unravel the story one step further by using genetics and neurobiological evidence.

Belief bias

The most interesting source of logical error, in my opinion, is the belie bias heuristic. It interests me for two reasons. First, the most important arguments are often made in the context of strongly held beliefs. Real-world, everyday reasoning is typically based in a system of beliefs and knowledge and the more important a decision, often the more emotionally charged it is. Second, the effect is strong and has been replicated in many types of deductive reasoning (e.g., categorical syllogistic (Evans, et al., 1983); conditional (Byrne and Tasso, 1999) and relational (Roberts and Sykes, 2003)) in many populations (children and adults with and without psychiatric disorder (de Jong et al., 1997; Handley et al., 2004). The belief-bias effect has been well studied for decades from a psychological perspective and has generated many hypotheses and theories in the field of reasoning. To this day, it amazes me that highly intelligent university students, despite explicit instruction to ignore beliefs and respond based on logic alone, consistently fall prey to belief bias. In my experience across several reasoning experiments (behavioral and fMRI), comparing performance on belief-congruent versus belief-incongruent trials consistently yields medium to large effect sizes (~0.4–0.5). In psychology, this is quite impressive! In sum, belief bias (and more recently, emotion) have been my main research focus and the tools I use to study them are largely from cognitive neuroscience and neurobiology, functional magnetic resonance imaging (fMRI) and genetics.

The belief-bias effect is increased by many factors, such as time pressure (Tsujii and Watanabe, 2010); additional cognitive demands (dual-task paradigm (Tsujii and Watanabe, 2009)) and development/ageing (i.e., both younger children (Handley, et al., 2004) and older adults have increased belief bias (De Neys and Van Gelder, 2009; Tsujii, Okada, and Watanabe, 2010)). Even in healthy, educated, intelligent adults who are explicitly instructed to base their decision on logic rather than beliefs, the belief-bias effect is still found (Stollstorff, Vartanian, et al., 2012). In short, we tend to be biased by our beliefs. What causes this effect? Why are we so tempted to go with beliefs rather than logic?

The inhibition hypothesis of belief bias

The inhibition hypothesis of belief bias posits that increased errors for incongruent reasoning problems are not caused by poor logical reasoning per se, rather by poor inhibitory control (De Neys and Franssens, 2009; Handley, et al., 2004; Houde et al., 2000; Moutier et al., 2006; Stollstorff, Vartanian, et al., 2012). When judging the validity of a conclusion, the participant must inhibit his or her prior knowledge to focus on the logic. Thus, belief-logic conflict requires decontextualization – a separation between previous knowledge and the information held in working memory – and therefore inhibition, to complete the task. A comparison of these reasoning tasks with classic inhibition tasks such as the famous Stroop task (Stroop, 1935) reveals that the tasks both test the same phenomenon – the ability to suppress one cognitive process in favor of another. In the Stroop task, participants are instructed to say the color of each word as fast as they can. When the words are congruent with the color in which they are printed (e.g., "blue" is printed in the color blue), participants do not find this task too difficult (they tend to accurately name the color and their response is relatively fast). However, when the words are incongruent with the color in which they are printed, (e.g., "yellow" is printed in the color red), participants are slower and less accurate in their response. They have difficulty suppressing the automatic process of reading (the prepotent response) in favor of the less automatic process of color naming. Conclusion evaluation tasks with belief-laden content share this inhibitory control component with the Stroop task and other classic inhibitory control tasks. In the belief-logic conflict condition, participants must inhibit their beliefs that are activated upon reading the conclusion (prepotent, automatic), to respond instead on the basis of logical validity (less automatic, more effortful). They must suppress one cognitive process, memory retrieval, in favor of another cognitive process, logical reasoning.

Not only does belief bias share essential cognitive task features with traditional inhibition tasks, it also relies upon the same brain region: the right lateral prefrontal cortex (rlPFC). Many methods have now converged upon the same result: fMRI studies find rlPFC to be active during successful belief-bias suppression (Goel and Dolan, 2003a; Stollstorff, Vartanian, et al., 2012); and disrupting the function of this region using repetitive transcranial magnetic stimulation (rTMS) impairs reasoning for incongruent trials (Tsujii et al., 2010). The evidence is quite convincing that the right lateral PFC, known to be recruited for classic inhibition tasks (Aron et al., 2004), is involved in belief-bias suppression.

Emotion and reason

The idea that emotion opposes logic ("reason versus passion"), dates back to ancient times of Aristotle and other great philosophers and is still widely accepted today. There is, however, surprisingly little empirical data to support this commonly held belief. In fact, recent studies in cognitive neuroscience have provided evidence to suggest that emotional factors facilitate the reasoning process through the ventromedial prefrontal cortex (vmPFC). Patients with damage to the vmPFC often have blunted or abnormal emotional responses and also seem to have difficulties in real-world decision-making (Anderson et al., 2006; Bechara et al., 2000;

Stuss et al., 1992). So perhaps emotion helps, or is even necessary for, successful reasoning.

The limited amount of empirical research on the effect of emotion on deductive reasoning has painted a different picture – one more in line with the "old fashioned" view of logic and emotion in opposition. Both affective content (words in the reasoning problem) and affective state ("mood") reduce logical reasoning performance (Blanchette, 2006; Blanchette and Richards, 2004; Lefford, 1946; Oaksford et al., 1996). Reasoning performance was lower for emotionally evoking statements, such as "War times are prosperous times, and prosperity is highly desirable, therefore, wars are much to be desired" (Lefford, 1946) or anxiety-related statements, such as "If there is danger, then one feels nervous" (Blanchette and Richards, 2004), relative to emotionally neutral statements and words, such as "All whales live in water and all fish live in water, therefore, all fish must be whales" or "If one eats a sandwich, then he is eating cheese". Furthermore, temporarily evoking negative or positive mood also reduces reasoning performance. Participants who were shown emotionally evoking pictures prior to reasoning made more errors in a conditional reasoning task (Wason selection task) than a control group who were shown emotionally neutral pictures (Oaksford, et al., 1996). Furthermore, anxiety, related to negative mood, also influences reasoning. Patients with specific phobias and non-clinical participants with high social anxiety had increased belief bias in deductive reasoning (de Jong et al., 1998; de Jong, et al., 1997; Vroling and de Jong, 2009). Thus, emotion (content and mood) can hinder the reasoning process. In terms of brain mechanisms, emotional reasoning recruits the ventromedial prefrontal cortex (vmPFC) rather than the more lateral prefrontal cortex typically engaged during non-emotional reasoning (Goel and Dolan, 2003b).

Serotonin transporter gene and emotional reactivity

The serotonin story is not a simple one, but it is certainly an important one as it relates to many aspects of human behavior and well-being (Canli and Lesch, 2007). Serotonin (5-hydroxytryptamine; 5-HT), a neurotransmitter synthesized in the raphe nucleus (brain stem), is released throughout the entire brain. The serotonin transporter protein (5-HTT), located on the pre-synaptic terminal of the neuron, is the main mechanism for termination of 5-HT action. It clears serotonin back to the pre-synaptic neuron, removing it from the synapse and thereby terminating its action.[2] There is a region in the serotonin transporter gene (SLC6A4) where a polymorphism occurs and this region is referred to as "5-HTTLPR" (Serotonin Transporter Long Promoter Region, or "SERT"). SERT influences 5-HTT mRNA transcription, which results in different levels of the 5-HTT protein (Hu et al., 2006). Our genetic code is quite brilliantly redundant, often containing sections that repeat many times. The short "S" allele, which repeats only 14 times, is linked to lower expression of serotonin transporter mRNA relative to the long "L" allele, which repeats 16 times (Hu et al., 2006). Further, the L allele contains an A to G single nucleotide polymorphism (SNP rs25531) that influences transcriptional efficiency, rendering the LG allele functionally similar to the S allele. Therefore, the SERT genetic polymorphism is actually "triallelic", meaning three alleles: S, LG, and LA. Since the LG allele is functionally equivalent to the S allele, we will simplify things and group the LG and S alleles together (S'), separate from the LA allele (L). We inherit two alleles, one from each parent, so an individual can be one of the following three genotypes: SS, SL, or LL.

SERT genotype influences emotional reactivity. Findings of studies comparing S carriers with homozygous L carriers (LL) suggest that the S allele is associated with higher emotional reactivity. First, genetic association studies suggest that the S allele contributes to risk for affective psychiatric disorders as it is over transmitted in those patients (Caspi, et al., 2003). Second, healthy carriers of the S allele scored higher on measures of depressive and anxiety-related behaviors (Gonda et al., 2009; Lesch et al., 1996; Lonsdorf et al., 2009). They also showed a stronger bias towards negative emotional content (e.g., angry faces) in an emotional dot probe task (Beevers et al., 2009; Perez-Edgar et al., 2010) and showed increased interference from negative stimuli (e.g., threat words or angry faces) in Stroop-like tasks (Koizumi et al., 2010). Third, numerous functional neuroimaging studies show that the amygdala, a critical brain region underlying emotional behavior, is more responsive to negative stimuli in healthy S carriers (Munafo et al., 2008; von dem Hagen et al., 2011). Together, these findings indicate that Short carriers differ in emotional reactivity from Long carriers, suggesting a "negativity bias" or heightened sensitivity for negative emotion.

In addition, evidence now suggests a "positivity bias" for the Long (LL) genotype (Fox et al., 2009; Perez-Edgar, et al., 2010). For example, in an emotional dot probe paradigm, Long carriers are more attracted to happy faces; that is, they tend to pay more attention to positive emotion. Groups did not differ in reaction to neutral faces. Furthermore, Stroop-like interference effects in the prefrontal cortex and posterior processing areas are increased by positive emotional content (happy faces) for the carriers of the Long/Long genotype (Stollstorff et al., 2013). In sum, the Short/Short individuals are more likely to detect fearful faces and other threats in the environment, whereas the Long/Long individuals are more likely to detect happy faces and positive environmental stimuli. The Long group "accentuates the positive" while the Short group seems to be primed to attend to threats and other negative emotional content.

What is the mechanism by which emotion interferes with logic? How does emotion interact with beliefs? If emotional reactivity reduces reasoning performance and a genetic polymorphism increases emotional reactivity, the genetic polymorphism ought to reduce reasoning performance. As I explained, emotional factors (for example, anxiety) relate to individual differences in deductive reasoning performance, and individual differences in anxiety are attributable, in part, to genetic polymorphisms. Thus, it is possible that genetics contribute to reasoning errors through individual differences in emotional reactivity. Consequently, in my studies I began by exploring a gene that has been linked to anxiety and other aspects of emotional reactivity (the serotonin transporter gene) to further our understanding of deductive reasoning and errors caused by emotionality and beliefs.

Beliefs, emotions and serotonin

I used to believe in the tooth fairy. When my brother disputed this belief, I did everything in my power to dissuade him from his erroneous position including resorting to violence and a massive crying fit. Our strongest beliefs can be the most resistant to change and providing evidence that logically contradicts the belief can evoke a strong emotional reaction. Are individuals who have stronger emotional reactivity more biased by their beliefs?

Evidence from my research suggests that this is indeed the case. Healthy adults were genotyped for SERT status (S/S, S/L or L/L). We excluded heterozygotes (carriers of both the S and L alleles) and included two groups in our reasoning experiment: Short (S/S carriers) and Long (L/L carriers). Participants completed a logical reasoning task to measure belief bias under two conditions: negative emotional content and emotionally neutral content. The participants' task was to determine whether the conclusion was logical or not logical, irrespective of their beliefs or knowledge about the truth or falsity of the conclusion. An example of an emotional problem: cockroaches are smaller than snakes; cockroaches are bigger than maggots; snakes are bigger than maggots. An example of a non-emotional problem: trees are taller than flowers; trees are shorter than grass; flowers are shorter than grass. Problems were either belief-logic congruent or belief-logic incongruent. A belief-bias index was calculated by the difference between performance for congruent and incongruent problems. Problems were logically identical across conditions; they only varied in the level of affective intensity (high or low negative affect) and in belief-logic congruency (congruent, incongruent).

As predicted, the Short group, associated with biased attention towards negative information, displayed higher belief bias in the emotional condition relative to the Long group; groups did not differ in the non-emotional condition (Stollstorff, Bean, et al., 2012). Furthermore, the Short group reported higher trait anxiety (STAI) (Spielberger et al., 1983) relative to the Long group; evidence that individuals in the Short group did perceive themselves to have higher negative affect. Anxiety was positively correlated with the level of emotional (but not non-emotional) belief bias (i.e., individuals with higher anxiety tended to have higher emotional belief bias). Thus, one's genetic predisposition towards negative affect influences the ability to reason logically in an emotional context.

What is the neural mechanism by which the serotonin transporter polymorphism influences belief bias? As described previously, a key region in reducing belief-bias susceptibility is the right lateral prefrontal cortex (rlPFC) (Goel and Dolan, 2003a; Stollstorff, Vartanian, et al., 2012; Tsujii, et al., 2010). To link the effect of SERT on emotional belief bias to previous brain studies, I needed to ascertain whether this key brain region, the rlPFC, is modulated by SERT during emotional belief-bias suppression. Participants were recruited for an fMRI study similar to the behavioral-genetic study described above; that is, two groups (Short or Long carriers) solving reasoning problems with emotional or non-emotional content that were either belief-logic congruent or incongruent. Since evidence had developed indicating that SERT Long homozygotes (L/L) have increased sensitivity to positive information, we included a positive emotional condition as well.

Neuroimaging results revealed a double dissociation in two key regions: the rlPFC and bilateral amygdala. Behavioral performance was quite high, likely due to a computer practice session prior to the experimental task, and groups did not differ in belief-bias performance accuracy or reaction time. However, differences were detected in the brain. The Short group required more activation of the rlPFC to overcome negative belief bias, while the Long group required more activation of this region to overcome positive belief bias. The same pattern of activity was found in the amygdala, and we interpret this as bottom-up reactivity to the positive and negative stimuli for Long and Short carriers, respectively. That is, the amygdala was more reactive to negative emotional content in Short carriers and more reactive to positive emotional content in Long carriers, requiring more top-down inhibitory control from rlPFC. Therefore, lower-level attentional bias towards or away from a specific emotional valence, caused by serotonin transporter genotype, can affect high-level thinking and reasoning via basic emotional and cognitive control brain regions (Stollstorff et al., in prep).

The studies I have discussed thus far involved healthy participants solving problems in a relatively emotionally neutral environment (i.e., no major threats, no major potential rewards). One might wonder what would happen if the emotional stakes were raised slightly? To begin to address this issue, we decided to set up an fMRI experiment similar to our behavioral-genetic study, in the sense that the context was more overwhelmingly negative. In this study, we contrasted negative and emotionally neutral problems only (excluding a positive valence condition), so that ~50 per cent of the material was negative. We targeted the negatively-biased Short group first, as this group is at risk for clinical disorder such as depression and anxiety (Caspi, et al., 2003). Our results showed that Short allele carriers had less involvement of the rlPFC and instead recruited the ventromedial prefrontal cortex (vmPFC) during emotional belief-logic conflict reasoning. Thus, they recruited a region of the brain that is involved with emotional processing rather than belief-logic conflict resolution, which could lead to decisions based on highly salient emotional beliefs, rather than logical reasoning. I propose that the negative context of the experiment caused a shift in the neural circuitry recruited by the Short carriers: from a "cool" logical lateral prefrontal network to a "hot" affective ventromedial network, perhaps more susceptible to emotionally biased reasoning. The idea is the following: for certain individuals (Short carriers), under higher demand (overwhelmingly negative context), the rlPFC "shuts down" and disengages, and the brain relies instead on an affective network more sensitive to heuristic biases and bottom-up emotional reactivity. Further research is necessary to test this hypothesis: (1) this study requires replication; (2) other manipulations of emotion could be made (for example, to test this in depressed patients or to evoke negative mood in healthy participants); and (3) the Long group should be tested under high positive demands to see if they, too, "break down" under high emotional demands and recruit affective brain networks rather than the cognitive right lateral prefrontal cortex.

Dopamine, inhibitory control and belief bias

Just as the serotonin transporter gene influences emotional reactivity, which in turn leads to increased belief bias, the dopamine transporter gene (DAT1) might also contribute to belief bias by influencing inhibitory control. If inhibitory control ability is the underlying process supporting belief-bias suppression, then genetic factors affecting cognitive control should in turn relate to individual differences in the ability to suppress belief bias.

Dopamine is thought to be a critical neurotransmitter supporting inhibitory control in the prefrontal cortex (Goldman-Rakic et al., 1992; Murphy et al., 1996). Various functional genetic polymorphisms influence dopamine function in the brain and thereby influence cognitive control, for example, the dopamine transporter gene (DAT1). The dopamine transporter protein (DAT) clears dopamine from the synapse and recycles it back up to the presynaptic terminal, thereby inactivating dopamine. Although DAT is distributed in many parts of the brain, including the PFC, the striatum (caudate, putamen and globus pallidus) has a particularly high DAT density (Lewis et al., 2001). The DAT polymorphism (DAT1) results in individual differences in DAT density in the brain. The two most common variants are the 9- and 10-repeat alleles. The 10-repeat allele is associated with more DAT and therefore less dopamine action at the synapse. Individuals inheriting two copies of the 10-repeat allele (10/10) have higher DAT density, a higher prevalence of ADHD, and lower performance on cognitive control tasks (Cook, et al., 1995; Cornish et al., 2005; Stollstorff et al., 2010; VanNess et al., 2005). Functional MRI studies have found effects of DAT1 on prefrontal activation during working memory tasks, with 10/10 individuals demonstrating less prefrontal activation (Bertolino et al., 2006). The 10/10 DAT1 genotype is also associated with impaired cognitive control and prefrontal-striatal-parietal function in children (Stollstorff, et al., 2010), a network of regions also found to be active during relational reasoning (Goel, 2007; Stollstorff and Vaidya, in prep).

In a recent study, we found that healthy adult carriers of the 10/10 genotype had increased belief bias relative to the 9/10 genotype. Furthermore, the 10/10 genotype group recruited the rlPFC to a lesser extent than did the 9/10 genotype group (Stollstorff and Vaidya, in prep). Thus, individuals inheriting the DAT1 10/10 genotype, which is associated with poor inhibitory control, have impaired ability to inhibit their beliefs in favor of logic. These data support the Inhibition Hypothesis of the belief-bias effect.

Preliminary data investigating the interaction between serotonin (SERT) and dopamine (DAT1) transporter genes on negatively valenced emotional belief-bias suppression indicate that carriers of *both* risk alleles (for negative emotional reactivity and poor inhibitory control: Short SERT and 10/10 DAT1, respectively) have significantly higher belief bias (~17 per cent belief-bias score) relative to the other genotype groups (~6 per cent belief-bias score). Although this finding will need to be replicated in a large-scale study, it is as would be predicted, since these individuals are more sensitive to the distracting negative emotional content and have less inhibitory control to suppress it in favor of logic. It highlights that gene x gene interaction could explain much more variance than a single gene alone.

Implications

Our work has important implications for studies of emotional reasoning. I have presented evidence that the serotonin transporter gene, known to influence attention towards or away from emotionally valenced information, can affect logical reasoning and the brain mechanisms that support this process. This is not to say that the (roughly) 20 per cent of us who carry this genotype cannot overcome our predisposition. However, we should be aware that certain environmental contexts or triggers might make it more difficult to reason logically for some individuals and could have the opposite effect for other individuals. For example, cognitive therapy for specific phobia that focuses on changing the patient's irrational fear of spiders might work better in a positive context for individuals who carry two copies of the SERT short allele, in light of their high sensitivity to negative context and resulting logic-resistant beliefs. But this same positive environment might have distracting and opposing effects for someone with the Long genotype. We can also see why some studies of the effect of emotion on reasoning might yield mixed results if valence and genotype are not taken into account.

Conclusion

Although we might have the potential for logical reasoning, humans do not always demonstrate this ability, as evidenced by errors in deductive reasoning tasks. Some of these errors are predictable and can be accounted for by known factors, such as belief bias. Some factors, such as emotion, that seem to predict patterns of reasoning error are at earlier stages of investigation. Still other factors that contribute to error variance are unknown. Genetics could help elucidate underlying mechanisms that promote or inhibit logical reasoning.

The emerging work that I presented in this chapter indicated that SERT and DAT1 influenced emotion-cognition interactions in brain function and behavior. It is fascinating that this small region of our DNA could actually relate to our ability to make rational decisions in the real world and thereby enhance or diminish our chances of survival. It is even more intriguing to consider the combination of genes that are known to have similar effects on cognition and emotionality. Future investigations of gene-gene interactions and their impact on rationality and emotionality look promising.

Notes

1 DNA extraction and genotyping are either processed "in house" (contact your nearest biology department), by a dedicated genetics laboratory in an academic research environment, or commercially.
2 For example, antidepressants, such as Prozac and Zoloft, work by blocking serotonin re-uptake by blocking the serotonin transporter (Huezo-Diaz et al., 2009).

References

Anderson, S. W., Barrash, J., Bechara, A. and Tranel, D. (2006). Impairments of emotion and real-world complex behavior following childhood- or adult-onset damage to ventromedial prefrontal cortex. *Journal of the International Neuropsychological Society: JINS*, *12*, 224–35.

Aron, A. R., Robbins, T. W. and Poldrack, R. A. (2004). Inhibition and the right inferior frontal cortex. *Trends in Cognitive Science*, *8*, 170–7.

Bechara, A., Tranel, D. and Damasio, H. (2000). Characterization of the decision-making deficit of patients with ventromedial prefrontal cortex lesions. *Brain*, *123*(*Pt 11*), 2189–202.

Beevers, C. G., Wells, T. T., Ellis, A. J. and McGeary, J. E. (2009). Association of the serotonin transporter gene promoter region (5-HTTLPR) polymorphism with biased attention for emotional stimuli. *Journal of Abnormal Psychology*, *118*, 670–81.

Bertolino, A., Blasi, G., Latorre, V., Rubino, V., Rampino, A., Sinibaldi, L., et al. (2006). Additive effects of genetic variation in dopamine regulating genes on working memory cortical activity in human brain. *Journal of Neuroscience*, *26*, 3918–22.

Blanchette, I. (2006). The effect of emotion on interpretation and logic in a conditional reasoning task. *Memory & Cognition*, *34*, 1112–25.

Blanchette, I. and Richards, A. (2004). Reasoning about emotional and neutral materials. Is logic affected by emotion? *Psychological Science*, *15*, 745–52.

Byrne, R. M. and Tasso, A. (1999). Deductive reasoning with factual, possible, and counterfactual conditionals. *Memory & Cognition*, *27*, 726–40.

Canli, T. and Lesch, K. P. (2007). Long story short: the serotonin transporter in emotion regulation and social cognition. *Nature Neuroscience*, *10*, 1103–9.

Caspi, A., Sugden, K., Moffitt, T. E., Taylor, A., Craig, I. W., Harrington, H., et al. (2003). Influence of life stress on depression: moderation by a polymorphism in the 5-HTT gene. *Science*, *301*, 386–9.

Cook, E. H., Jr., Stein, M. A., Krasowski, M. D., Cox, N. J., Olkon, D. M., Kieffer, J. E., et al. (1995). Association of attention-deficit disorder and the dopamine transporter gene. *American Journal of Human Genetics*, *56*, 993–8.

Cornish, K. M., Manly, T., Savage, R., Swanson, J., Morisano, D., Butler, N., et al. (2005). Association of the dopamine transporter (DAT1) 10/10-repeat genotype with ADHD symptoms and response inhibition in a general population sample. *Molecular Psychiatry*, *10*, 686–98.

de Jong, P. J., Haenen, M. A., Schmidt, A. and Mayer, B. (1998). Hypochondriasis: the role of fear-confirming reasoning. *Behaviour Research and Therapy*, *36*, 65–74.

de Jong, P. J., Mayer, B. and van den Hout, M. (1997). Conditional reasoning and phobic fear: evidence for a fear-confirming reasoning pattern. *Behaviour Research and Therapy*, *35*, 507–16.

De Neys, W. and Franssens, S. (2009). Belief inhibition during thinking: not always winning but at least taking part. *Cognition*, *113*, 45–61.

De Neys, W. and Van Gelder, E. (2009). Logic and belief across the lifespan: the rise and fall of belief inhibition during syllogistic reasoning. *Developmental Science*, *12*, 123–30.

Domchek, S. M., Friebel, T. M., Singer, C. F., Evans, D. G., Lynch, H. T., Isaacs, C., et al. (2010). Association of risk-reducing surgery in BRCA1 or BRCA2 mutation carriers with cancer risk and mortality. *JAMA: the Journal of the American Medical Association*, *304*, 967–75.

Egan, M. F., Goldberg, T. E., Kolachana, B. S., Callicott, J. H., Mazzanti, C. M., Straub, R. E., et al. (2001). Effect of COMT Val108/158 Met genotype on frontal lobe function and risk for schizophrenia. *Proceedings of the National Academy of Sciences of the United States of America, 98*, 6917–22.

Evans, J. S., Barston, J. L. and Pollard, P. (1983). On the conflict between logic and belief in syllogistic reasoning. *Memory & Cognition, 11*, 295–306.

Fox, E., Ridgewell, A. and Ashwin, C. (2009). Looking on the bright side: biased attention and the human serotonin transporter gene. *Proceedings of Biological Science, 276*, 1747–51.

Frayling, T. M., Timpson, N. J., Weedon, M. N., Zeggini, E., Freathy, R. M., Lindgren, C. M., et al. (2007). A common variant in the FTO gene is associated with body mass index and predisposes to childhood and adult obesity. *Science, 316*, 889–94.

Goel, V. (2007). Anatomy of deductive reasoning. *Trends in Cognitive Sciences, 11*, 435–41.

Goel, V., Buchel, C., Frith, C. and Dolan, R. J. (2000). Dissociation of mechanisms underlying syllogistic reasoning. *NeuroImage, 12*, 504–14.

Goel, V. and Dolan, R. J. (2003a). Explaining modulation of reasoning by belief. *Cognition, 87*, B11–22.

Goel, V. and Dolan, R. J. (2003b). Reciprocal neural response within lateral and ventral medial prefrontal cortex during hot and cold reasoning. *NeuroImage, 20*, 2314–21.

Goldman-Rakic, P. S., Lidow, M. S., Smiley, J. F. and Williams, M. S. (1992). The anatomy of dopamine in monkey and human prefrontal cortex. *Journal of Neural Transmission. Supplementum, 36*, 163–77.

Gonda, X., Fountoulakis, K. N., Juhasz, G., Rihmer, Z., Lazary, J., Laszik, A., et al. (2009). Association of the s allele of the 5-HTTLPR with neuroticism-related traits and temperaments in a psychiatrically healthy population. *European Archive of Psychiatry and Clinical Neuroscience, 259*, 106–13.

Handley, S. J., Capon, A., Beveridge, M., Dennis, I. and Evans, J. S. B. (2004). Working memory, inhibitory control and the development of children's reasoning. *Thinking and Reasoning, 10*, 175–95.

Houde, O., Zago, L., Mellet, E., Moutier, S., Pineau, A., Mazoyer, B., et al. (2000). Shifting from the perceptual brain to the logical brain: the neural impact of cognitive inhibition training. *Journal of Cognitive Neuroscience, 12*, 721–8.

Hu, X. Z., Lipsky, R. H., Zhu, G., Akhtar, L. A., Taubman, J., Greenberg, B. D., et al. (2006). Serotonin transporter promoter gain-of-function genotypes are linked to obsessive-compulsive disorder. *American Journal of Human Genetics, 78*, 815–26.

Huezo-Diaz, P., Uher, R., Smith, R., Rietschel, M., Henigsberg, N., Marusic, A., et al. (2009). Moderation of antidepressant response by the serotonin transporter gene. *British Journal of Psychiatry, 195*, 30–8.

Koizumi, A., Kitagawa, N., Kitamura, M. S., Kondo, H. M., Sato, T. and Kashino, M. (2010). Serotonin transporter gene and inhibition of conflicting emotional information. *NeuroReport, 21*, 422–6.

Lefford, A. (1946). The influence of emotional subject matter on logical reasoning. *Journal of General Psychology, 34*, 127–51.

Lesch, K. P., Bengel, D., Heils, A., Sabol, S. Z., Greenberg, B. D., Petri, S., et al. (1996). Association of anxiety-related traits with a polymorphism in the serotonin transporter gene regulatory region. *Science, 274*, 1527–31.

Lewis, D. A., Melchitzky, D. S., Sesack, S. R., Whitehead, R. E., Auh, S., and Sampson, A. (2001). Dopamine transporter immunoreactivity in monkey cerebral cortex: regional, laminar, and ultrastructural localization. *The Journal of Comparative Neurology*, 432, 119–36.

Lonsdorf, T. B., Weike, A. I., Nikamo, P., Schalling, M., Hamm, A. O. and Ohman, A. (2009). Genetic gating of human fear learning and extinction: possible implications for gene-environment interaction in anxiety disorder. *Psychological Science*, *20*, 198–206.

Luo, J., Yuan, J., Qiu, J., Zhang, Q., Zhong, J. and Huai, Z. (2008). Neural correlates of the belief-bias effect in syllogistic reasoning: an event-related potential study. *NeuroReport*, *19*, 1073–8.

Moutier, S., Plagne-Cayeux, S., Melot, A. M. and Houde, O. (2006). Syllogistic reasoning and belief-bias inhibition in school children: evidence from a negative priming paradigm. *Developmental Science*, *9*, 166–72.

Munafo, M. R., Brown, S. M. and Hariri, A. R. (2008). Serotonin transporter (5-HTTLPR) genotype and amygdala activation: a meta-analysis. *Biological Psychiatry*, *63*, 852–7.

Murphy, B. L., Arnsten, A. F., Goldman-Rakic, P. S. and Roth, R. H. (1996). Increased dopamine turnover in the prefrontal cortex impairs spatial working memory performance in rats and monkeys. *Proceedings of the National Academy of Sciences of the United States of America*, *93*, 1325–9.

Oaksford, M., Morris, F., Grainger, B. and Williams, J. M. G. (1996). Mood, reasoning, and central executive processes. *Journal of Experimental Psychology: Learning, Memory, and Cognition*, *22*, 476–92.

Perez-Edgar, K., Bar-Haim, Y., McDermott, J. M., Gorodetsky, E., Hodgkinson, C. A., Goldman, D., et al. (2010). Variations in the serotonin-transporter gene are associated with attention bias patterns to positive and negative emotion faces. *Biological Psychology*, *83*, 269–71.

Prado, J., Chadha, A. and Booth, J. R. (2011). The brain network for deductive reasoning: a quantitative meta-analysis of 28 neuroimaging studies. *Journal of Cognitive Neuroscience*, *23*, 3483–97.

Roberts, M. J. and Sykes, E. D. (2003). Belief bias and relational reasoning. *Quarterly Journal of Experimental Psychology*, *56*, 131–53.

Rowe, D. C., Stever, C., Giedinghagen, L. N., Gard, J. M., Cleveland, H. H., Terris, S. T., et al. (1998). Dopamine DRD4 receptor polymorphism and attention deficit hyperactivity disorder. *Molecular Psychiatry*, *3*, 419–26.

Spielberger, C. D., Gorsuch, R. L., Lushene, R., Vagg, P. R. and Jacobs, G. A. (1983). *Manual for the State-Trait Anxiety Inventory: STAI (Form Y)*. Palo Alto, CA: Consulting Psychologists Press.

Stollstorff, M., Banich, M., Smolker, H., Jensen, A., Guild, R., Devaney, J. M., et al. (in prep). Overcoming emotional interference for logical reasoning: an fMRI study of serotonin transporter genotype effects on amygdala and inferior prefrontal cortex activity.

Stollstorff, M., Bean, S. E., Anderson, L. M., Devaney, J. M. and Vaidya, C. J. (2012). Rationality and emotionality: serotonin transporter genotype influences reasoning bias. *Social Cognitive and Affective Neuroscience*, *8*(4), 404–409.

Stollstorff, M., Bean, S., Parrot, W. N., Anderson, L. M., Devaney, J. M., and Vaidya, C. J. (in prep). Serotonin transporter genotype and negative emotional content influence prefrontal recruitment during belief-bias suppression in relational reasoning.

Stollstorff, M., Foss-Feig, J., Cook, E. H., Jr., Stein, M. A., Gaillard, W. D. and Vaidya, C. J. (2010). Neural response to working memory load varies by dopamine transporter genotype in children. *NeuroImage*, *53*, 970–7.

Stollstorff, M., Munakata, Y., Smolker, H., Jensen, A., Guild, R., Devaney, J. M., et al. (2013). Individual differences in emotion-cognition interactions: emotional valence interacts with serotonin transporter genotype to influence brain systems involved in emotional reactivity and cognitive control. *Frontiers in Human Neuroscience*, *7*, 327

Stollstorff, M., Vartanian, O. and Goel, V. (2012). Levels of conflict in reasoning modulate right lateral prefrontal cortex. *Brain Research*, *1428*, 24–32.

Stroop, J. R. (1935). Studies of interference in serial verbal reactions. Ph D, George Peabody College for Teachers, George Peabody College for Teachers, Nashville, TN.

Stuss, D. T., Gow, C. A. and Hetherington, C. R. (1992). "No longer Gage": frontal lobe dysfunction and emotional changes. *Journal of Consulting and Clinical Psychology*, *60*, 349–59.

Tsujii, T., Masuda, S., Akiyama, T. and Watanabe, S. (2010). The role of inferior frontal cortex in belief-bias reasoning: an rTMS study. *Neuropsychologia*, *48*, 2005–8.

Tsujii, T., Okada, M. and Watanabe, S. (2010). Effects of aging on hemispheric asymmetry in inferior frontal cortex activity during belief–bias syllogistic reasoning: A near-infrared spectroscopy study. *Behavioural Brain Research*, *210*(2), 178–183.

Tsujii, T. and Watanabe, S. (2009). Neural correlates of dual-task effect on belief-bias syllogistic reasoning: a near-infrared spectroscopy study. *Brain Research*, *1287*, 118–25.

Tsujii, T. and Watanabe, S. (2010). Neural correlates of belief-bias reasoning under time pressure: a near-infrared spectroscopy study. *NeuroImage*, *50*, 1320–6.

Van Ness, S. H., Owens, M. J. and Kilts, C. D. (2005). The variable number of tandem repeats element in DAT1 regulates in vitro dopamine transporter density. *BMC Genetics*, *6*, 55.

von dem Hagen, E. A., Passamonti, L., Nutland, S., Sambrook, J. and Calder, A. J. (2011). The serotonin transporter gene polymorphism and the effect of baseline on amygdala response to emotional faces. *Neuropsychologia*, *49*, 674–80.

Vroling, M. S. and de Jong, P. J. (2009). Deductive reasoning and social anxiety: evidence for a fear-confirming belief bias. *Cognitive Therapy Research*, *33*, 633–44.

Waldman, I. D., Rowe, D. C., Abramowitz, A., Kozel, S. T., Mohr, J. H., Sherman, S. L., et al. (1998). Association and linkage of the dopamine transporter gene and attention-deficit hyperactivity disorder in children: heterogeneity owing to diagnostic subtype and severity. *American Journal of Human Genetics*, *63*, 1767–76.

Walker, F. O. (2007). Huntington's disease. *Seminars in Neurology*, *27*, 143–50.

3 The rationality of mortals

Thoughts of death disrupt analytic processing

Bastien Trémolière and Jean-François Bonnefon

Summary

Thinking about death triggers defensive mechanisms that use up executive resources, which are no longer available for demanding mental tasks such as logical reasoning, moral judgment, and probabilistic thinking. This chapter reviews evidence for the disruptive effect of death thoughts on various reasoning tasks, and speculates on the reason why we humans came to be aware of our future death, only to try not to think about it, at a significant cognitive cost.

Introduction

Knowing that you are going to die is probably the ultimate feat of reasoning. It is a strange recursive trick of consciousness, to reach the abstract conclusion that one day consciousness will stop forever. Maybe not as a coincidence, human mortality features prominently in the most well-known logical syllogism of all: Socrates is a man, all men are mortals, therefore Socrates is mortal. It would seem that death, with the famed certainty it shares with taxes, and its by-design abstract character, would be an ideal content for purely analytical, abstract, logical thinking. Ironically, just the opposite is true. The idea we will develop in this chapter is that thinking about death prevents us from putting our analytical skills to use, and deactivates our ability for abstract reasoning. The deep irony here (and we will return to it in the conclusion) is that the very skills (e.g., analytic thinking) that led us to discover the truth about our future death are the first skills that the thought of death deactivates, every time it occurs to us.

We begin with a short introduction mixing two literatures on thinking: mortality salience (thinking about death) and dual-process models (thinking fast and slow). In this section we lay out our main claim: thinking about death triggers defensive mechanisms that use up executive resources, which are no longer available for analytical reasoning.[1] In three subsequent sections, we examine the empirical case for this claim in three domains where analytical thinking can be deployed: logical reasoning, moral reasoning and probabilistic reasoning. Finally, we look at some big questions in the conclusion: does the detrimental effect of death thoughts on cognitive processing mean we are bound to make bad decisions on all problems of life and death? And if it is so cognitively costly not to think about death, why do we know about it in the first place – or conversely, if it was adaptive for us to know about death, why do we sacrifice so many cognitive resources not to think about it?

Death and dual processes

We worry about many things in the course of a typical day: errands we might forget, papers we have not read, children we should monitor – and common sense would suggest that the greater the disutility of a future event, the more we worry about it. Curiously though, we do not usually spend much time worrying about death, even though the disutility of dying is magnitude larger than that of the other things we worry about. According to terror management theory (Greenberg, Pyszczynski and Solomon, 1986) and the hundreds of research papers it inspired (see for reviews Burke, Martens and Faucher, 2010; Hayes, Schimel, Arndt and Faucher, 2010), the conspicuous absence of death among our daily concerns results from the efficacy of various cognitive mechanisms, whose function is to help us escape the paralyzing anxiety brought up by the prospect of dying.

More specifically, the dual-process formulation of terror management theory (Pyszczynski, Greenberg and Solomon, 1999) postulates that reminders of death trigger a two-stage reaction of denial. In the first stage, executive resources are mobilized to suppress thoughts of death, i.e., to banish them out of conscious awareness (a feat that apparently takes five or ten minutes). Once this is achieved, another phase starts whose aim is to bolster self-esteem in order to provide a buffer against the potential anxiety generated by the now preconscious thoughts of death. We will not concern ourselves with this second phase, and will focus instead on what happens immediately after one is reminded of his or her inescapable death. In laboratory experiments, this reminder typically takes the form of the mortality salience manipulation. Subjects are invited to write a few lines in response to the two following questions:

> Briefly describe the emotions that the thought of your own death arouse in you. Jot down, as specifically as you can, what you think will happen as you physically die and once you are physically dead.

Terror management theory assumes that immediately after this manipulation, subjects mobilize executive resources in order to push thoughts of death outside of consciousness (for a review of though suppression mechanisms, see Wenzlaff and Wegner, 2000). This assumption allows for one general and straightforward prediction: whichever mental activity requires executive resources, will be impaired immediately after a mortality salience manipulation (Arndt, Greenberg, Solomon, Pyszczynski and Simon, 1997; Gailliot, Schmeichel and Baumeister, 2006).

This prediction of terror management theory meshes well with the dual-process approach to reasoning, judgment and decision-making (Evans, 2008; Kahneman, 2011). A considerable literature established that logical problems (Evans, 2007), moral dilemmas (Greene, 2007) and decision problems (Kahneman and

Fredericks, 2005) can be solved either by automatic or analytical processing, that analytical processing requires executive resources, and that the response that is ultimately produced tracks the type of processing which was engaged during its production.

In the following sections, we take advantage of this framework to test one general prediction: mortality salience disrupts analytical processing, across logical, moral and probabilistic reasoning. We consider in turn logical syllogisms, moral dilemma and probabilistic judgments, and review data suggesting in each case a disruption of analytical processing by mortality salience.

Death and syllogisms

The belief-bias task (Evans, Barston and Pollard, 1983) is a typical paradigm used by cognitive psychologists as well as neuroscientists to investigate dual-process accounts of reasoning. Responses on the belief-bias task reliably track the engagement of executive resources for analytical processing (De Neys, 2006).

The belief-bias task involves solving (in particular) so-called *incongruent* problems with a logically valid but unbelievable conclusion, or an invalid but believable conclusion. Here is an example of a typical incongruent problem, with a valid but unbelievable conclusion:

1 a. No healthy person is unhappy;
b. There are unhappy persons who are astronauts;
c. Therefore, there are astronauts who are not healthy.

The task is to assess the logical validity of the conclusion, here (1-c), as a function of the two premises, here (1-ab). In this example, the intuitive response is that the conclusion is invalid, since most people would hold the belief that all astronauts are very healthy individuals. A rigorous consideration of the problem, however, shows that the conclusion can be logically derived from the premises. Rejecting a valid conclusion because of its unbelievability, or accepting an invalid conclusion because of its believability, is a display of the belief-bias effect. The belief bias is particularly persistent and difficult to overcome, even when instructions strongly emphasize the need to approach the task logically (Evans, Newstead, Allen, and Pollard, 1994).

Critically, dual process theorists assume that overcoming the intuitive but logically incorrect response to incongruent problems requires that executive resources be deployed. In line with this assumption, normative performance on the belief-bias task correlates with cognitive capacity and is impaired by cognitive load (De Neys, 2006). Therefore, any context that can divert a part of reasoners' limited cognitive resources is likely to impair performance on incongruent problems. According to our general claim, mortality salience can provide such a context.

Following this rationale, Trémolière, De Neys and Bonnefon (in press) invited reasoners to solve syllogisms (that included incongruent problems) immediately after they were reminded of their mortality, by way of a French version of the mortality salience manipulation. Half the subjects went through the classic mortality salience manipulation:

> Briefly describe the emotions that the thought of your own death arouse in you. Jot down, as specifically as you can, what you think will happen as you physically die and once you are physically dead.

The other participants responded to similar questions, except that they referred to extreme pain instead of death:

> Briefly describe the emotions that the thought of extreme pain arouse in you. Jot down, as specifically as you can, what you think will happen as you endure extreme pain and once you have endured extreme pain.

This control group was used to ensure that the effects of mortality salience were not solely driven by virtue of eliciting negative affect. The prediction was that reasoners who thought of death would reason less logically on incongruent problems, compared to reasoners who thought of extreme pain. And indeed this is what happened. Only 59 per cent of responses were logical when reasoners answered under mortality salience, compared to the 72 per cent logical responses given by reasoners who thought about extreme physical pain.

In another experiment, the effect of mortality salience was compared with that of a classic concurrent load manipulation, the spatial storage task known as the Dot Memory task (Bethell-Fox and Shepard, 1988; Miyake, Friedman, Rettinger, Shah, and Hegarty, 2001). This task has already been shown to draw on executive resources, and to impair logical performance on the incongruent problems of the belief-bias task. It involves briefly flashing up to subjects (before every problem) a 3 × 3 matrix in which some cells are filled with dots. Subjects must memorize the location of the dots. Once they have evaluated the syllogism, participants see an empty matrix and must fill it with dots in order to reproduce the initial configuration.

The dot memory task is known to impair logical performance on incongruent problems, and it did so in this experiment. The disrupting effect of mortality salience was also replicated. The interesting finding of this experiment, though, came from the participants who were both under mortality salience and under concurrent cognitive load. These participants had to respond to the two death-thoughts inducing questions, and then had to memorize the dot patterns before they solved each syllogism.

These participants (and only these participants) showed elevated death-thought accessibility at the end of the experiment. The classic death-thought accessibility measure invites subjects to complete words in which two consecutive letters are missing. Some of these words have two possible completions, one related to death, and one that is not. For example, COFF__ has two completions, one that is related to death (COFFIN) and one that is not (COFFEE). The greater the number of death-related completions, the more the subject is considered to think about death at the moment of measurement.

Reasoners usually thought very little about death at the end of the experiment (5 to 10 per cent death-related completions), but for one notable exception. Reasoners who went through the mortality salience manipulation and the concurrent load task had a much greater score on the death accessibility task (about 30 per cent death related completions). It appears that concurrent cognitive load impaired the suppression of death thoughts: when cognitively burdened (and only when cognitively burdened), participants under mortality salience thought more about death at the end of the experiment.

Other experiments ruled out alternative explanations for the effect of mortality salience on reasoning. For example, subjects were given the 10-item version of the Rational-Experiential Inventory (Epstein, Pacini, Denes-Raj and Heier, 1996), as well as the Positive and Negative Affect Schedule (PANAS) (Watson, Clark and Tellegen, 1988), at the beginning and at the end of the experiment. The mortality salience manipulation did not impact the thinking mode of the subjects, nor their affective state.

These results support the claim that death thought suppression eats up cognitive resources, as evidenced by people's performance at logical reasoning. Mortality salience decreases logical performance on the belief-bias task, presumably because it diverts executive resources to the suppression of death thoughts, at the expense of analytical thinking.

Death and morality

Moral judgment has long been construed as a highly thoughtful, reflective mental activity (Kohlberg, 1969; Turiel, 1983), only to be later recast as a primarily intuitive, emotion-based affair (Blair, 1995; Haidt, 2001; Nichols, 2002). The dual process approach to moral judgment (Greene, Sommerville, Nystrom, Darley and Cohen, 2001; Greene, Nystrom, Engell, Darley and Cohen, 2004) conjoins these two perspectives, by assuming that different responses to moral dilemma track the engagement of either one of two mental processes. Consider for example the famous footbridge dilemma:

> A trolley is hurtling down a track towards five people. You are on a bridge under which it will pass, and you can stop it by dropping a heavy weight in front of it. As it happens, there is a very fat man next to you – your only way to stop the trolley is to push him over the bridge and onto the track, killing him to save five. Should you proceed?

According to the dual process theory of moral judgment, the utilitarian response (yes, it is acceptable to push the man in order to save the five) results from the engagement of analytical processing, whereas the deontic response (no, it is unacceptable to push the man, regardless of the consequences of this action) reflects the engagement of emotional, non-analytical processing. The utilitarian response would thus require us to engage executive resources – and according to our general claim, it should therefore be less likely to be given as a response under mortality salience.

Indeed, following the same reasoning as in the previous section, it can be expected that mortality salience will shape moral judgment and decrease the likelihood of producing utilitarian judgments in responses to moral dilemma such as the footbridge problem. As we will argue in the final section of this chapter, this is an important matter because difficult moral questions often involve issues of life and death. It is therefore highly significant that the very nature of these mortality related issues might shape moral judgments by preventing reasoners from giving them their full analytical attention (regardless of whether an analytical response is ethically best or not).

To investigate this claim, Trémolière, De Neys and Bonnefon (2012) ran a series of experiments in which participants had to judge the moral acceptability of different decisions immediately after a mortality salience manipulation. Importantly, they used a moral dilemma which involved non-lethal harm, such as the following version of the Crying Baby dilemma:

> Leo is a civilian during the war. He and his six children are hidden in the cellar of their house. If the enemy sees them, they will all be captured and tortured. The youngest child is still a baby. Enemy soldiers are searching the house when the baby starts to cry. Leo puts his hand over the baby's mouth so that the noise does not attract the enemy soldiers' attention. The only possibility for Leo not to get caught with his children is to leave his hand on the baby's mouth, which will deprive him of air for a few minutes and will have serious consequences on his mental and respiratory systems. Is it morally acceptable that Leo decides to smother his baby in order to save his five other children from torture?

It was necessary to use non-lethal harm versions of the dilemma in these experiments in order to ensure that they would not intrinsically evoke thoughts of death. This way, it was possible to assess the effect of the mortality salience, by comparing the judgments of subjects who thought about death immediately before reading the dilemma, to that of subjects who thought about pain. It was expected that subjects who thought about death would show less utilitarian judgments than subjects who thought about pain, and this is what happened. Under mortality salience 49 per cent of the judgments were utilitarian, compared to the 72 per cent utilitarian judgments given by subjects who thought about pain. Thus supporting the view that thoughts of death influence moral judgments.

Another experiment aimed at comparing the effect of mortality salience to that of the dot matrix task (i.e., different load levels). It has been a straightforward prediction of the dual-process account that concurrent cognitive load would impact on the frequency of utilitarian judgments, but this prediction had not yet been confirmed. Our findings indicate that the effect of mortality salience is comparable to that of an extreme cognitive load (i.e., moderate load did not have an impact on the frequency of utilitarian judgments). Indeed, it would thus appear that previous attempts designed to elicit this effect (Greene, Morelli, Lowenberg, Nystrom and Cohen, 2008) used too weak a manipulation of concurrent load. Utilitarian judgments do appear to require executive resources, but not as much as it was previously hypothesized: one needs a very strong manipulation of concurrent load to impact them, a fact that will have to be considered in future research.

In an additional, unpublished experiment conducted in our laboratory, we sought to find evidence that the mere contents of the moral dilemma might elicit a mortality salience effect (i.e., the contents featured death rather than non-lethal harm). Thus, rather than using an exogenous mortality salience manipulation, we simply invited subjects to respond to either the non-lethal harm version of the dilemma (see above), or to a life-and-death version, for example:

> Leo is a civilian during war. He and his six children are hidden in the cellar of their house. If the enemy sees them, they will all be captured and killed. The youngest child is still a baby. Enemy soldiers are searching the house when the baby starts to cry. Leo puts his hand over the baby's mouth so that the noise does not attract the enemy soldiers' attention. The only possibility for Leo not to get caught with his children is to leave his hand on the baby's mouth, which will deprive him of air for a few minutes and will choke him to death.

Results were in line with our expectations, and with the results obtained with an exogenous mortality salience manipulation. Participants who saw the lethal versions of the dilemma were less utilitarian (52 per cent) than those who saw their non-lethal harm version (64 per cent).[2] It is thus a very real possibility that a situation involving life and death might intrinsically elicit a mortality salience effect and consequently shape moral judgments through the disruption of analytical processing. This claim, however, is currently undergoing further experimental scrutiny.

Death and probabilities

We have reviewed evidence suggesting that mortality salience prompts individuals to allocate executive resources to the suppression of death thoughts, at the expense of analytical thinking. The third domain to which we can export this general hypothesis is that of probabilistic reasoning. There are many tasks in the domain of judgment and decision-making which are known to track the engagement of analytical processing, and mortality salience should affect them just as it affects logical and moral reasoning. Many such tasks are currently under investigation at our research group, among them probability matching, base rate neglect and the conjunction fallacy.

A typical probability matching problem, adapted from West and Stanovich (2003), would read as follows:

> A die with four red faces and two green faces will be rolled six times. Before each roll you will be asked to predict which color (red or green) will show up once the die is rolled. Which color is most likely to show up after roll #1? after roll #2? . . . after roll #6?

When each correct prediction is rewarded, the strategy that maximizes gains is to always bet on red, since red has a greater probability of occurrence on any given roll. It can be tempting, though, to make predictions that match the probabilities of red and green, by betting four times on red and two times on green. Executive resources are presumably involved in overcoming this temptation and adopting the maximizing strategy (Stanovich and West, 2008).

If mortality salience diverts executive resources to the suppression of death thoughts, it should make it harder for reasoners to adopt the maximizing strategy. This is what our ongoing work would seem to demonstrate: about 25 per cent of reasoners adopted the maximizing strategy under mortality salience, compared to 35 per cent in the control (pain) group. A different version of the task, involving cards instead of dice, replicated this finding.

Our investigations of the conjunction fallacy and of base rate neglect failed so far to demonstrate a general effect of mortality salience. These two tasks showed such a low rate of analytical responding in our control groups that a ceiling effect presumably prevented the detection of the mortality salience effect. This interpretation is supported by the fact that participants of very high cognitive ability, as measured by their score on the cognitive reflection test (Fredericks, 2005), did show impaired performance under mortality salience – but still better performance than participants of lesser cognitive ability. Further research will thus be necessary in order to extend our demonstrations to the field of judgment and decision-making.

Conclusions and speculations

The findings we reviewed in this chapter make a strong case for the claim that thoughts of death impair analytical processing. In this final section, we consider two questions raised by this conclusion. First, it is not the first time that some factor is identified that disrupts analytical processing – so, why should we grant special importance to mortality salience in that respect? Second, can our results shed new light on the evolutionary enigma of death awareness – that is, what could possibly be the benefits of knowing that we are going to die?

Why is it so important?

Analytic processing can be impaired by depletion of a variety of resources, from time (Evans and Curtis-Holmes, 2005; Suter and Hertwig, 2011) over cognitive fatigue (Gailliot et al., 2007), to serotonin (Crockett, Clark, Tabibnia, Lieberman and Robbins, 2008). So, is mortality salience just one more manipulation among many? We think that it is not the case. We believe instead that the mortality salience effect is especially important, for three reasons: it can be huge, it is presumably ubiquitous in everyday life, and its chief targets are, by design, matters of life and death.

The sheer size of the mortality salience effect is remarkable on its own. In our experiments on logical reasoning, we observed that the effect size of the mortality salience manipulation was much greater than that of a typical concurrent load manipulation. In our experiments on moral reasoning, we found out that it took a concurrent load manipulation of unprecedented strength to equal the effect of mortality salience. In sum, the simple fact of thinking of one's death is sufficient to inflict mental load greater or equal to that of carefully crafted laboratory manipulations.

Besides its sheer size, the effect of mortality salience is likely to be encountered frequently in everyday life. Empirical studies of the availability of death thoughts have shown that many events can remind individuals of their mortality, and bring thoughts of death to focal attention or implicit pre-attention (Hayes et al., 2010). It is plausible (although speculative) that executive resources will be mobilized whenever thoughts of death sit at the border of consciousness, or become readily conscious. This would mean that the disruptive effect of death thoughts could be encountered in every context that serves as a reminder of death, and these contexts are legion. Indeed, it has been shown that death thoughts increase in availability when people think about illnesses such as cancer (Arndt, Cook, Goldenberg and Cox, 2007), when they think about old age (Martens, Greenberg, Schimel and Landau, 2004), but also when they think about physical sex (Goldenberg, Pyszczynski, Greenberg and Solomon, 2000), or, for women, when they perform a breast self-examination (Goldenberg, Arndt and Hart, 2008). Death thoughts are also made available when people hear about the risk of driving (Jessop, Albery and Garrod, 2008), the risks of smoking (Hansen, Winzeler, and Topolinski 2010), or about terrorism and conflicts (Vail, Arndt, Motyl and Pyszczynski, 2012). Even if it is probably too vast and too complex a research endeavor, it would be useful to know exactly how frequently people are led to think about death in any given day (and, by implication, how often they could potentially be impaired in their thinking) – the figure would quite likely be staggering.

Not only is the detrimental effect of mortality salience large and frequent, but it is likely to specifically impact high-stakes situations. By definition, mortality salience is associated with contexts that involve death. Health decisions are a prime example of these, as well as risky behaviors. Clearly, it is especially concerning that such contexts might, by design, trigger a mechanism that deprives individuals of the executive resources they would otherwise deploy to reach a thoughtful understanding of the situation. One is also led to worry about the fact that mortality salience would disrupt thoughtful moral reasoning, given the fact that questions involving life and death have risen at the forefront of contemporary ethics. This has been thoroughly examined by the philosopher Peter Singer (1994) who suggests that advances in the biomedical sciences have led to the collapse of traditional ethics. Not only do many countries struggle with continuing moral debates involving abortion and euthanasia, but technological advances have brought entirely novel issues to professional and public attention. In other words, although preoccupation with death-related issues are nothing new in ethics, our technologically advanced environment is rapidly transforming the nature of these issues.

Consider, for example, the very problem of defining what death is. A traditional (and intuitive) definition would identify death with the cessation of breathing and blood circulation in the body. In modern times, though, these two bodily functions can be preserved artificially for an extraordinary length of time and for patients for whom there is no chance that they ever regain consciousness. Should hospital space and resources be directed to keeping these patients alive, or redirected to other patients? In parallel, the possibility of heart transplantation has led to an even thornier dilemma. One can only transplant viable organs, and the heart is no longer viable when blood in the donor's body has stopped circulating. According to the intuitive definition of death, heart transplantation would therefore require that the doctor remove the heart from a living donor – that is, to commit murder. One way out of this dilemma would be to redefine death, so that it would officially occur at some point when the heart is still viable (but after brain activity has irreversibly stopped). This is what was done in most countries with the capacity for heart transplantation.

As shown by this example, our modern world is ripe with ethical dilemmas that involve life and death, and for which we have no answer at the ready – because these dilemmas did not exist until technology created them. We will not claim that analytical processing is required to attain a satisfactory resolution of these dilemmas, as it is, how could such a claim be tested? We believe, however, that it cannot be a good thing that analytical processing should be impaired by the very nature of these dilemmas, and that mortality salience should unduly shape private opinion and public debates on such important topics. We therefore call for a wide research effort aimed at understanding how mortality salience might disrupt our understanding of life-and-death ethical dilemma borne out of biomedical advances – and we also call for a wide research effort directed at providing interventions for analytical processing so that it can better stand its place in the public understanding of these dilemmas.

How did it come to be?

Why do we know that we are going to die? The question here is not about the mechanism by which we reach this knowledge, but about the evolutionary, functional reason for such knowledge. It is tempting to imagine that since we all naturally come to know about death, this ability has to be an adaptation. But what then would be the fitness advantages that would come with knowing that death is upon us? Some speculate that just as fear is an adaptation in response to specific threats, the anxiety that comes with the prospect of death is the drive that makes us go the extra-mile to survive (Humphrey, 2011). However, it is hard to reconcile this view with the fact which has been referred to again and again in this chapter: that we spend so much effort and executive resources to *not* think about death.

According to terror management theory, the reason for all these efforts is that the awareness of death can potentially provoke debilitating anxiety. The word *debilitating* is key here, since fear and anxiety normally are adaptive responses, whose continuous and effortful inhibition would be counterproductive. Why would the fear of death be subject to continuous inhibition, but not the fear of snakes or the fear of heights (Navarrete and Fessler, 2005)? It seems hard to find a plausible way out of the horns of the anxiety dilemma: if death anxiety is good, fitness-wise, then there would be no point in combating it so fiercely and at such a cognitive cost. One could imagine that there could exist a sweet spot of death anxiety, which we would be carefully engineered to experience, at a tremendous cost of executive resources. It is hard to believe that evolution would not have stumbled upon a more efficient solution, though.

A way out of this dilemma is to recast the problem in order to avoid the reference to anxiety. Let us start with the possibly trivial assumption that higher-level cognition is a tremendous evolutionary advantage. With higher-level cognition, though, comes as a trade off the awareness of death (Landau, Solomon, Pyszczynski, and Greenberg, 2007). Now let us say that the risk attached to the awareness of death is not debilitating anxiety, but rather existential despair: that the knowledge of death would not paralyze us with anxiety, but would slowly deprive us of the will to live – that our effortful denial of death is not aimed at preserving us from anxiety, but at preserving us from suicide. Denial of death would turn out to be a clever trick from our genes, which would give us the illusion that we share their own temporal horizon, and which would discourage us to leave the game early on.

Now we can recast the problem as an evolutionary arms race between increased cognitive abilities and an increased propensity to suicide. Maybe there has been a critical time in the evolutionary history of humanity, when the denial of death was late compared to the cognitive ability to know about death. Maybe entire branches of humanity have reached evolutionary bottlenecks because they have evolved the ability to know about death, without having evolved the ability not to think about death, as vividly imagined by Humphrey (2011). We must admit that we have no idea of how such grand claims might be tested scientifically: we are making extensive use of the license given to us by the editors of this book, to forget all typical restraints in the final section of our chapter, and to give free rein to our most speculative thoughts. Without as much as a hint on how to proceed, we can only hope that future research on death and cognition will lay bare the evolutionary history of that tragic aspect of being human: having come to know about death, only to frenetically try not to know about it.

Notes

1 In this chapter, we adopt a simple operational definition of analytical thinking: analytical thinking is such that it loads to a significant extent on executive resources.

2 The effect is not as large as in our other experiments, but note that the mortality salience manipulation is also less direct. It is unlikely that *all* subjects were prompted to think about their own death when reading the lethal version of the dilemma.

References

Arndt, J., Cook, A., Goldenberg, J. and Cox, C. (2007). Cancer and the threat of death: The cognitive dynamics of death thought suppression and its impact on behavioral health intentions. *Journal of Personality and Social Psychology*, *92*, 12–29.

Arndt, J., Greenberg, J., Solomon, S., Pyszczynski, T. and Simon, L. (1997). Suppression, accessibility of death-related thoughts, and cultural worldview defense: Exploring the psychodynamics of terror management. *Journal of Personality and Social Psychology, 73*(1), 5–18.

Bethell-Fox, C. E. and Shepard, R. N. (1988). Mental rotation: Effects of stimulus complexity and familiarity. *Journal of Experimental Psychology: Human Perception and Performance, 14*, 12–23.

Blair, R. J. R. (1995). A cognitive developmental approach to morality: Investigating the psychopath. *Cognition, 57*, 1–29.

Burke, B. L., Martens, A. and Faucher, E. H. (2010). Two decades of terror management theory: a meta-analysis of mortality salience research. *Personality and Social Psychology Review, 14*, 155–195.

Crockett, M., Clark, L., Tabibnia, G., Lieberman, M. D. and Robbins, T. (2008). Serotonin modulates behavioral reactions to unfairness. *Science, 320*, 1739.

De Neys, W. (2006). Dual processing in reasoning: Two systems but one reasoner. *Psychological Science, 17*, 428–433.

Epstein, S., Pacini, R., Denes-Raj, V. and Heier, H. (1996). Individual differences in intuitive-experiential and analytical-rational thinking styles. *Journal of Personality and Social Psychology, 71* (2), 390–405.

Evans, J. S. B. T. (2007). *Hypothetical thinking: Dual processes in reasoning and judgment*. New York: Psychology Press.

Evans, J. S. B. T. (2008). Dual-processing accounts of reasoning, judgment, and social cognition. *Annual Review of Psychology, 59*, 255–278.

Evans, J. S. B. T., Barston, J. L. and Pollard, P. (1983). On the conflict between logic and belief in syllogistic reasoning. *Memory and Cognition, 11*, 295–306.

Evans, J. S. B. T. and Curtis-Holmes, J. (2005). Rapid responding increases belief bias: Evidence for the dual-process theory of reasoning. *Thinking and Reasoning, 11*, 382–389.

Evans, J. S. B. T., Newstead, E., Allen, J. and Pollard, P. (1994). Debiasing by instruction: The case of belief bias. *European Journal of Cognitive Psychology, 6* (3), 263–285.

Fredericks, S. (2005). Cognitive reflection and decision making. *Journal of Economic Perspectives, 19*, 25–42.

Gailliot, M. T., Baumeister, R. F., DeWall, C. N., Maner, J. K., Plant, E. A., Tice, D. M., et al. (2007). Self-control relies on glucose as a limited energy source: Willpower is more than a metaphor. *Journal of Personality and Social Psychology, 92*, 325–336.

Gailliot, M. T., Schmeichel, B. J. and Baumeister, R. F. (2006). Self-regulatory processes defend against the threat of death: Effects of self-control depletion and trait self-control on thoughts and fears of dying. *Journal of Personality and Social Psychology, 91*, 49–62.

Goldenberg, J. L., Arndt, J. and Hart, J. (2008). Uncovering an existential barrier to breast self-exam behavior. *Journal of Experimental Social Psychology, 44*, 260–274.

Goldenberg, J. L., Pyszczynski, T., Greenberg, J. and Solomon, S. (2000). Fleeing the body: A terror management perspective on the problem of human corporeality. *Personality and Social Psychology Review, 4*, 200–218.

Greenberg, J., Pyszczynski, T. and Solomon, S. (1986). The causes and consequences of a need for self-esteem: A terror management theory. In R. F. Baumeister (Ed.), *Public self and private self* (pp. 189–212). New York: Springer-Verlag.

Greene, J. D. (2007). Why are VMPFC patients more utilitarian? A dual-process theory of moral judgment explains. *Trends in Cognitive Sciences, 11*, 322–323.

Greene, J. D., Morelli, S. A., Lowenberg, K., Nystrom, L. E. and Cohen, J. D. (2008). Cognitive load selectively interferes with utilitarian moral judgment. *Cognition, 107*, 1144–1154.

Greene, J. D., Nystrom, L. E., Engell, A. D., Darley, J. M. and Cohen, J. D. (2004). The neural bases of cognitive conflict and control in moral judgment. *Neuron, 44*, 389–400.

Greene, J. D., Sommerville, R. B., Nystrom, L. E., Darley, J. M. and Cohen, J. D. (2001). An fmri investigation of emotional engagement in moral judgment. *Science, 293*, 2105–2108.

Haidt, J. (2001). The emotional dog and its rational tail. *Psychological Review, 108*, 814–834.

Hansen, J., Winzeler, S. and Topolinski, S. (2010). When the death makes you smoke: A terror management perspective on the effectiveness of cigarette on-pack warnings. *Journal of Experimental Social Psychology, 46*, 226–228.

Hayes, J., Schimel, J., Arndt, J. and Faucher, E. H. (2010). A theoretical and empirical review of the death-thought accessibility concept in terror management research. *Psychological Bulletin, 136*, 699–739.

Humphrey, N. (2011). *Soul dust: the magic of consciousness*. London: Quercus.

Jessop, D. C., Albery, I. P. and Garrod, J. R. H. (2008). Understanding the impact of mortality-related health-risk information: A terror management theory perspective. *Personality and Social Psychology Bulletin,34*, 951–964.

Kahneman, D. (2011). *Thinking, fast and slow*. New York: Farrar, Straus and Giroux.

Kahneman, D. and Fredericks, S. (2005). A model of heuristic judgement. In K. J. Holyoak and R. G. Morrison (Eds.), *The Cambridge handbook of thinking and reasoning* (pp. 267–293). Cambridge, MA: Cambridge University Press.

Kohlberg, L. (1969). Stage and sequence: The cognitive-developmental approach to socialization. In D. A. Goslin (Ed.), *Handbook of socialization theory and research* (pp. 347–480). Chicago: Rand McNally.

Landau, M., Solomon, T., Pyszczynski, T. and Greenberg, J. (2007). On the compatibility of terror management theory and perspectives on human evolution. *Evolutionary Psychology, 5*, 476–519.

Martens, A., Greenberg, J., Schimel, J. and Landau, M. (2004). Ageism and death: Effects of mortality salience and similarity to elders on distancing from and derogation of elderly people. *Personality and Social Psychology Bulletin, 30*, 1524–1536.

Miyake, A., Friedman, N. P., Rettinger, D. A., Shah, P. and Hegarty, M. (2001). How are visuospatial working memory, executive functioning, and spatial abilities related? A latent-variable analysis. *Journal of Experimental Psychology: General, 130*, 621–640.

Navarrete, D. and Fessler, D. (2005). Normative bias and adaptive challenges: A relational approach to coalitional psychology and a critique of terror management theory. *Evolutionary Psychology, 3*, 297–325.

Nichols, S. (2002). Norms with feeling: Towards a psychological account of moral judgment. *Cognition, 84* (2), 221–236.

Pyszczynski, T., Greenberg, J. and Solomon, S. (1999). A dual-process model of defense against conscious and unconscious death-related thoughts: An extension of terror management theory. *Psychological Review, 106*, 835–845.

Singer, P. (1994). *Rethinking life and death: the collapse of our traditional ethics*. Oxford: Oxford University Press.

Stanovich, K. and West, R. (2008). On the relative independence of thinking biases and cognitive ability. *Journal of Personality and Social Psychology, 94* (4), 672–695.

Suter, R. S. and Hertwig, R. (2011). Time and moral judgment. *Cognition, 119*, 454–458.

Trémolière, B., De Neys, W. and Bonnefon, J. F. (in press). The grim reasoner: Analytical reasoning under mortality salience.

Trémolière, B., De Neys, W. and Bonnefon, J. F. (2012). Mortality salience and morality: Thinting about death makes people less utilitarian. *Cognition, 124*, 379–384.

Turiel, E. (1983). *The development of social knowledge: Morality and convention.* Cambridge, MA: Cambridge University Press.

Vail, K. E., Arndt, J., Motyl, M. and Pyszczynski, T. (2012). The aftermath of destruction: Images of destroyed buildings increase support for war, dogmatism, and death thought accessibility. *Journal of Experimental Social Psychology*, *48*, 1069–1081.

Watson, D., Clark, L. A. and Tellegen, A. (1988). Development and validation of brief measures of positive and negative affect: the panas scales. *Journal of Personality and Social Psychology*, *54* (6), 1063–1070.

Wenzlaff, E. M. and Wegner, D. M. (2000). Thought suppression. *Annual Review of Psychology*, *51*, 59–91.

West, R. F. and Stanovich, K. E. (2003). Is probability matching smart? Associations between probabilistic choices and cognitive ability. *Memory and Cognition, 31* (2), 243–251.

4 Negative priming in logicomathematical reasoning

The cost of blocking your intuition

Grégoire Borst, Sylvain Moutier and Olivier Houdé

Summary

A large number of studies have provided converging evidence that humans are biased when they reason. Some argue that these reasoning errors are committed because of a failure to detect the conflict between intuitive responses and normative considerations while others argue that systematic errors in logical tasks reflect difficulty in resisting (inhibit) interference from heuristic thinking. In this chapter, we introduce the 'negative priming' paradigm, a method that we believe can provide evidence that inhibitory processes are involved in situations in which conflicts in reasoning strategies arise. In the final part of the chapter, we outline how this method can be successfully adapted to reasoning paradigms in order to provide evidence that inhibitory control is critical to thinking rationally.

Introduction

Human brains, unlike the brains of other mammals, have the distinctive characteristic of enabling us to reason in a logical way (Goel et al., 1997, 1998; Piaget, 1984). According to Aristotle, the core feature of the human mind is the 'logos' which encompasses both reason (logic) and language. Similarly, Piaget (1984) proposed that the last stage of cognitive development is the stage of formal logical thinking. That is, deductive reasoning emerges from adolescence during the formal operation stage. However, one of the critical challenges for the human mind is to implement deductive rules to overcome reasoning errors by preventing heuristic thinking interference. Contemporary psychological studies of reasoning and decision-making have provided evidence that most adults are often biased when they reason (Evans, 1989, 1998; Houdé, 2000). Biases can be explained by the fact that people tend to rely overwhelmingly on their intuitions and on overlearned strategies (or heuristics) rather than on more cognitive demanding analytical strategies to make decisions (Houdé, 1997b).

Some authors have argued that heuristic biases arise essentially because of a failure to detect the conflict between intuitive responses and logical considerations (Kahneman and Frederick, 2002). However, others have proposed that reasoning biases stem from the inability to inhibit intuitive heuristic responses and not from the inability to detect conflicts between intuition and logic per se (De Neys, Vartanian and Goel, 2008; Epstein, 1994; Houdé, 1997b, 2007 but see Klauer, Musch and Naumer, 2000 for a non-dual process account of reasoning biases). Houdé, Moutier and colleagues have provided behavioral (Moutier and Houdé, 2003; Moutier, Plagne-Cayeux, Melot and Houdé, 2006) and neuroimaging (Houdé et al., 2000, 2001) evidence in support of the inhibition account. It suggests that systematic errors in logical tasks reflect difficulty with resisting (inhibiting) the interference between heuristic and analytic responses rather than an inability to grasp the underlying logic of the task at hand, or to detect the conflict between logic and belief.

For instance, at a behavioral level, Houdé and Moutier (1996, 1999; Moutier and Houdé, 2003) have demonstrated that executive training in inhibition of heuristic biases enables individuals to overcome these biases and think logically. One such task in which the effects of executive training were examined was the conditional rule falsification task. When participants are asked to falsify a conditional rule such as '*if there is not a red square on the left, then there is a yellow circle on the right*', most of them erroneously choose the two geometrical figures stated in the rule instead of selecting a true antecedent (not a red square, e.g., a blue diamond) and a false consequent (not a yellow circle, e.g., a green square). According to Evans (1972), the error is a result of a perceptual matching bias which is a process of simply matching items mentioned in the rule to the examples that participants must choose from in order to falsify the statement. In Houdé and Moutier's (1996, 1999) studies, participants first solved the conditional rule falsification task, and then received either bias inhibition training, logical training or no training on a different conditional reasoning task, the Wason card selection task (Wason, 1968). Finally, on the posttest they were presented with the same conditional rule falsification task as in the pretest. In the inhibition training condition, participants were trained to inhibit the matching bias by encouraging them to refrain from focusing exclusively on the number and the letter mentioned in the rule. In the logical training condition, the same training procedure was used without the inhibition component.[1] In the no training condition, participants simply performed the Wason task. Inhibition training was the only training condition that improved participants' reasoning performance on the posttest. In addition, brain-imaging studies revealed a shift from activation of the posterior part of the brain when participants gave biased responses to activation of a prefrontal network (comprising regions known to be associated with inhibitory control) when the same participants gave logical responses after the inhibition training phase (Houdé et al., 2000, 2001). This suggests that people are not irrational per se but are probably inefficient inhibitors in situations in which their heuristics conflict with logical knowledge.

The aim of this chapter is to outline how 'negative priming', a methodological approach widely used to reveal inhibitory control in situations in which information is in conflict, can be adapted to reasoning paradigms in order to provide direct evidence that inhibitory control is critical to think rationally. In the first section we will briefly present seminal negative priming studies and theoretical accounts of the negative priming effect. In the second section we review the few studies that have started applying the negative priming paradigm to classical syllogistic and other logicomathematical reasoning tasks. In the final section, we clarify how this methodology constitutes a promising approach to unravel the nature of reasoning errors.

Negative priming: generality, theoretical accounts and neuroimaging data

Generality of negative priming

In natural environments, we are confronted with more information than we can possibly process. Irrelevant information needs to be ignored in order to efficiently process relevant information. However, providing evidence of inhibitory control is difficult. One way of obtaining evidence of inhibitory control is by using a priming paradigm (e.g., negative priming). The experimental logic of the negative priming approach is as follows: if an item was previously ignored (or inhibited), then the subsequent processing of that item will be disrupted as revealed by slower or less accurate responses (see, e.g., Neill, Valdesand Terry, 1995; Tipper, 2001). In the classical negative priming paradigm, participants performed pairs of stimuli. The first stimulus of the pair is the prime; the second one is the probe. Classically, participants' performance is measured on the second stimulus (i.e., probe). Critically, performance is compared between test-probes in which the target is a distractor inhibited on the first stimulus (i.e., prime) and control-probes in which the target bears no relation with a distractor inhibited on the prime. For instance, participants will be slower to identify the central letter on the probe (e.g., HHH-CHHH), when preceded by a prime in which the target letter was a distractor (e.g., CCCBCCC) than when preceded by a prime in which the target letter was not a distractor (e.g., VVVBVVV). Negative priming is observed when the responses times or the number of errors is greater on the test than on the control probes. In some studies, an item can be a probe relative to the preceding trial and the prime relative to the next trial while in other studies prime-probe pairs are separated by a temporal window.

Negative priming effects were first reported in a Stroop (1935) task (Dalrymple-Alford and Budayr, 1966). In the Stroop task, participants are asked to name as quickly as possible the ink color of printed color words (e.g., BLUE). Participants typically require more time to identify the ink color when the ink color conflicts with the color denoted by the word (e.g., BLUE written in yellow ink) than when the two colors are congruent (e.g., BLUE written in blue ink) – i.e., the so-called 'Stroop effect'. In addition to the classical 'Stroop effect', Dalrymple-Alford and Budayr (1966) observed a negative priming effect. They reported that color naming was even slower when the word referred to the ink color of the item in the subsequent trial, say on trial 1 BLUE in yellow ink is presented, then trial 2 GREEN in blue ink, followed by trial 3 RED in green ink and so on. According to Dalrymple-Alford and Budayr (1966), participants were slower to perform such list of items because the color that needed to be named on a given item was ignored (inhibited) on the previous item.

Negative priming is not restricted to the Stroop task and has been reported in picture, word and letter identification tasks (e.g., Kane, Hasher, Stoltzfus, Zachs and Connelly, 1994; Tipper, 1985; Tipper and Cranston, 1985), in semantic and lexical categorization tasks (e.g., Tipper and Driver, 1988; Neely, 1977), in letter and shape matching tasks (e.g., DeShepper and Treisman, 1991; Neill, Lissner and Beck, 1990;), in counting tasks (e.g., Driver and Tipper, 1989), and in localization tasks (e.g., Tipper, Brehaut and Driver, 1990).

To illustrate the variety of tasks in which negative priming has been demonstrated, we focus on Tipper's (1985) seminal negative priming study. On each trial an object drawn in green ink was superimposed on an object drawn in red ink (e.g., a green cow on a red hammer). Target objects were always the red objects. Green objects served as distractors. Participants were instructed, on the prime (e.g., a green hat on a red chair) to identify the red object (e.g., chair) without naming it and, on the probe (e.g., a green shoe on a red hat), to name the red object (e.g., hat) as fast as possible. Then, participants were asked to report the name of the object in red presented on the prime to make sure that they identified it correctly. When the probe target (e.g., red hat) was identical to the prime distractor (e.g., green hat), participants required more time to respond than when the target object on the probe (e.g., red hat) was different from the distractor object on the prime (e.g., green cow). Negative priming is not restricted to perceptual similarities between the objects. Tipper (1985, Experiment 3) reported a similar negative priming effect when the probe target was not identical but semantically related to the prime distractor – for instance when a picture of a dog (in red on the probe) followed a picture of a cat (in green on the prime).

Similarly, negative priming was reported in a Stroop-like counting tasks (Driver and Tipper, 1989). On each trial, an array of the same digit (e.g., '2') was presented and participants were instructed to count the number of digits in the array. When the number of digits (e.g., '4') was in conflict with the digits presented (e.g., '2') participants required more time to respond than when the number of digits (e.g., '2') was congruent with the digits displayed in the array (i.e., a typical 'Stroop effect'). In addition, when participants counted four 2s on the prime, they were slower to count two 5s on the probe (i.e., a typical negative priming effect).

Finally, Tipper, Brehaut and Driver (1990) demonstrated that negative priming is not restricted to the inhibition of the identity of an object but also generalizes to the location of this object. In the negative priming location task, a target (e.g., X) and a distractor (e.g., O) object are presented on four possible locations (e.g., _ X _ O). Participants are instructed to press one out of four buttons to indicate the target object location. Participants were slower to indicate the position of the probe target when the position was the position occupied by the distractor on the prime (e.g., O _ _ X).

To conclude, negative priming is a robust effect reported with a variety of stimuli (word, picture, letter, number, location) and a variety of response modalities (vocal, button-press, reaching). This effect seems to generalize over identification, categorization, matching, counting, and localization. Although there is little doubt that negative priming exists, there are multiple theoretical accounts of this effect.

Principal theoretical accounts of negative priming

Nowadays at least two major models have been proposed to account for negative priming, the 'selective inhibition' (e.g., Houghton and Tipper, 1994; Houghton, Tipper, Weaver and Shore, 1996) and the 'episodic retrieval' (e.g., Neill and Valdes, 1992) models. We will briefly sketch these accounts here for completeness. The interested reader can find a more complete overview and the rife debate between them in Tipper (2001).

Selective inhibition

According to the 'selective inhibition' account, negative priming occurs because the mental representation of the ignored information (i.e., distractor) is actively inhibited on the prime in order to further process the mental representation of the selected information (i.e., target). Consequently, the response to the probe target is disrupted because the target to process corresponds to information that has been inhibited on the prime, and overcoming the inhibition (or blockage) of this information has a cognitive cost reflected by the increase in response times or errors on the probe. Note that this model assumes that at first both mental representations of attended and ignored information are activated and only then ignored information is inhibited on the prime (e.g., Tipper and Cranston, 1985). In sum, the critical feature of this model is that negative priming is due to the inhibition of interfering information on the prime.

Episodic retrieval

As opposed to the 'selective inhibition' account which assumes that the source of the negative priming is to be found during the encoding (i.e., on the prime), the 'episodic retrieval' account assumes that the source of this effect should be attributed to the retrieval process – the probe acting as a cue for memory retrieval (e.g., Neill and Valdes, 1992). According to the 'episodic retrieval' model, the target stimulus on the probe cues automatically the retrieval of previous processing episodes of this stimulus. These episodes contain information of previous processing of the stimulus such as its identity or location, and whether the stimulus is relevant or irrelevant. Stimuli that are encountered as distractors are associated with a 'do not respond' tag. Participants require more time to respond to an item on the probe if that item was previously associated with a 'do not respond' tag – i.e., distractor on the prime – because of a conflict between two processing episodes: the one on the prime and the one on the probe. This model differentiates itself from the 'selective inhibition' model by assuming that the inhibition of irrelevant information on the prime is not necessary to observe negative priming. However, inhibition is required on the probe because of the conflict between the processing episodes. The episodic retrieval model has the advantage that it provides an explanation for a number of experimental phenomena that are hard to account for in the selective inhibition model (e.g., why the absence of a distractor on the probe diminishes negative priming, see Neill, 1997). However, a major problem for the 'episodic retrieval' model is that it is hardly impossible to falsify it because it can always explain new data by assuming new tags (Tipper, 2001).

Other models have been put forward to explain negative priming such as the feature mismatching model (e.g. Park and Kanwisher, 1994) or the temporal discrimination model (e.g., Milliken, Joordens, Merikel and Seiffert, 1998). The presentation of these models falls beyond the scope of this review, but see Fox (1995) and Tipper (2001) for more details on these alternative theoretical accounts.

Neuroimaging studies of negative priming

Neuroimaging studies have started to investigate the neural underpinning of the negative priming effect in order to shed light on the underlying processes that produce negative priming. Electrophysiological studies have reported enhanced N200 in a flanker-like task (Frings and Groh-Bordin, 2007), a digit (Gibbons, 2006), and a letter (Ruge and Naumann, 2006) localization negative priming tasks. In all studies, increased negativity of the N200 wave was observed on a fronto-central location when the target on the probe was one of the distractors on the prime as compared to a control condition (i.e., a condition where the target on the probe was not related to the distractor on the prime). Furthermore, in a flanker-like negative priming study with letters – a target letter was flanked by two distracting letters (e.g., ABA) – the N200 was the only electrophysiological correlate of negative priming (Hinojosa, Pozo, Méndez-Bértolo and Luna, 2009). Given that the N200 component is viewed as reflecting response inhibition and cognitive control (e.g., Bartholow et al., 2005; Neuiwenhuis, Yeung, van den Wildenberg and Ridderinkhof, 2003), these studies provide evidence that inhibition is at play on the prime to prevent further processing of the distractors.

However, an additional component, the P300 on centro-parietal sites, has also been identified in negative priming tasks. As for the N200 component, the P300 amplitude is larger in test compare to control trials in negative priming experiments (e.g., Kathmann, Bogdahn and Endrass, 2006; Gibbons, 2006). The P300 component is related to both attentional processes (Donchin, Karis, Bashore, Coles and Gratton, 1986) and updating of information in memory (Polich and Kok, 1995). Some authors have argued that the modulation of the P300 in negative priming tasks could reflect the retrieval process of past processing episodes of the stimuli (e.g., Gibbons, 2006). fMRI studies revealed that a distributed network of regions is responsible for negative priming (e.g., Egner and Hirsh, 2005; Krueger, Fisher, Heineke and Hagendorf, 2007; Steel et al., 2001; Wright et al., 2006). In a Stroop negative priming task, activation was greater in the frontal and temporal lobes in a negative priming condition (i.e., the color of the ink on the probe corresponded to the color word on the prime) as compared to the degree of activation in a condition in which the color of the ink on the probe was unrelated to the color word presented previously (Steel et al., 2001). The activated frontal areas comprised regions such as the inferior frontal gyrus known to be involved in inhibitory control (see Aron, Robbins and Poldrack 2004; Houdé et al., 2010) whereas temporal activations probably reflected retrieval of past processing episodes of the stimuli (see Nyberg, 1998). In a location-based negative priming study, activations within the dorsolateral prefrontal cortex (DLPFC) and the inferior parietal lobule (IPL) were reported when the location of the target on the probe was the location previously occupied by a distractor on the prime (Krueger et al., 2007). According to the authors, the DLPFC serves as a top-down control and modulates activity in the IPL in order to select appropriate information when relevant and irrelevant information compete for attentional resources.

In sum, as behavioral data, neuroimaging data does not clearly validate one negative priming account over the other. As noted by Tipper (2001), 'selective inhibition' and 'episodic retrieval' models of negative priming can be distinguished essentially by the degree of emphasis they put on respectively the encoding stage on the prime vs. the retrieval process triggered by the probe. These two accounts are therefore not mutually exclusive. There is now little doubt that inhibitory control is required on the prime to prevent distractors to interfere with the processing of the target. Similarly, the target on the probe most likely triggers the retrieval of past processing episodes of this stimulus and if this stimulus was previously to be ignored, the interference between the present and the past processing episodes necessarily requires some sort of inhibitory control.

Negative priming in reasoning studies

In the final section of this chapter, we will review the studies that used negative priming to demonstrate that inhibitory control is necessary to reason logically. The logic of these studies is strictly identical to the ones presented in the previous section except that a strategy (or a system of beliefs) rather than a stimulus is assumed to be inhibited on the prime: If to reason logically one needs to inhibit an overlearned strategy or heuristic to activate a logical algorithm, then a negative priming effect should be observed when participants perform prime-probe sequences in which the heuristic that needs to be activated on the probe was inhibited on the prime. Bluntly put, if people block the heuristic response on one trial, they will pay a price if they need to rely on it on the subsequent trial.

Following this logic, Houdé and Guichart (2001) devised the first negative-priming paradigm to demonstrate that inhibitory control was required when children correctly solved a classic logicomathematical task – Piaget's number-conservation task (Piaget, 1952). In this task, first two rows with equal numbers of objects and equal lengths are presented to the children. Then, one of the rows is transformed in length – objects are spread apart – but not in the number of objects. Before the age of 7, children erroneously think that the longer row contains more objects. According to neo-Piagetian researchers (e.g., Houdé, 2000), the number-conservation task is an interference task in which a misleading visuospatial strategy (i.e., the length-equals-number heuristic) must be inhibited to activate the appropriate numerical strategy (Houdé, 1997a). To provide evidence of inhibitory control in the number-conservation task, Houdé and Guichart (2001) asked children to perform two types of prime-probe trials. In test trials, two rows of different length but with the same number of objects (i.e., a classical number-conservation item) was presented as the prime. In order to correctly state that the two rows contained the same number of objects, children had to inhibit the length-equals-number strategy. On the probe, an item in which length and number co-varied – i.e., the longer row contained more objects – was displayed (see Figure 4.1). Critically, the length-equals-number strategy that was inhibited on the prime became the appropriate strategy to activate on the probe. In control trials, the strategy to be used on the prime was unrelated to the strategy to activate on the probe. Objects were displayed in such a way that counting each object was the only appropriate strategy (i.e., the objects on one of the rows were displayed vertically on the screen which ruled out using the length-equals-number strategy). As on the test trials, an item in which length and number co-varied was displayed on the probe. Comparison of the probe response times between test and control trials revealed a clear negative priming effect (see Figure 4.1): children were slower to use the length-equals-number strategy after they performed a typical Piaget-like number-conservation item in which the length-equals-number strategy needed to

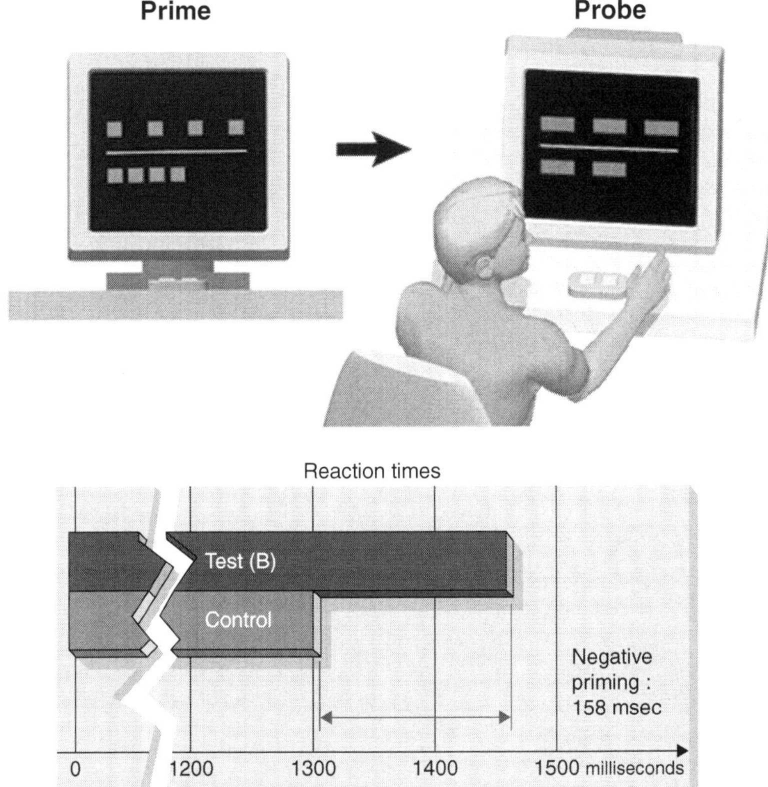

Figure 4.1 Procedure used on test trials in the negative priming adaptation of the number-conservation task (top). Response times in ms in control and test trials (bottom). Adapted from Houdé and Guichart, 2001.

be inhibited to overcome the interference between the length of the rows and the number of objects. This result suggests that children's ability to reason correctly on number conservation tasks is directly related to their ability to inhibit a misleading strategy.

In a follow-up electrophysiological study using a similar negative priming adaptation of the number-conservation task with young adults, Daurignac, Houdé and Jouvent (2006) reported enhanced amplitude of the N200 (with a large distribution over the scalp) when the length-equals-number strategy inhibited on the prime became the appropriate strategy to activate on the probe. Given that the N200 is assumed to reflect inhibitory control, electrophysiological data garnered in this study suggest that adults as children need to inhibit the length-equals-number heuristic to reason correctly here

Negative priming has also been reported in another logicomathematical Piagetian task, the class-inclusion task (Inhelder and Piaget, 1964). In this task, ten daisies (i.e., the subordinate class A) and two roses (i.e., the subordinate class A') are presented to the child and he(she) is asked whether there are more daisies than flowers (i.e., the superordinate class B=A+A'). Before the age of 7, children erroneously think that there are more daisies than flowers because they fail to perform the appropriate comparison between the superordinate class (flowers) and the subordinate class (daisies). To succeed at this task, children need to inhibit the direct perceptual comparison of the visuospatial extensions (the number of displayed elements) of the two subclasses (A and A') in order to activate the appropriate logical (or conceptual) comparison of the superordinate class (B) to its subordinate class (A). In the negative priming adaptation of the class-inclusion task (see Figure 4.2), adults and ten-year-old children performed test and control trials with three types of items: class-inclusion items, subclasses-comparison items, and control items (Borst, Poirel, Pineau, Cassotti and Houdé, 2013). Stimuli consisted of two rows of various geometric shapes of different colors separated by a horizontal line (e.g., 8 green squares and 4 blue squares). Class-inclusion items (e.g., "More green squares than squares": yes or no?) required to compare the superordinate class (e.g., squares) to one of its subordinate classes (e.g., green squares). Subclasses-comparison items required to compare the number of elements in the two subclasses (e.g., "More green squares than blue squares"). On control items participants were required to judge whether all objects had the same given property (e.g., "Squares have the same color"). In the test trials, participants performed a typical class-inclusion item on the prime (in which inhibition of the comparison of the subordinate classes' extensions was needed) and then a subclasses-comparison item on the probe (in which the direct comparison of the two subclasses' extensions became the appropriate strategy, e.g., comparing the number of blue and green squares). In the control trials, participants performed a control item on the prime followed by a subclasses-comparison item on the probe. Critically, the strategy to be used on the prime was not related to the strategy to be used on the probe. Negative priming was reported for both children and adults: children and adults were slower to determine that there were more objects in one subordinate class than in the other after they successfully determined that there were more elements in the superordinate class than in one of the two subordinate classes. In addition, negative priming decreased with age (see Figure 4.2). As a side-note, we would like to mention that the results reported in this study extend the related findings of Perret, Paour and Blaye (2003) in school-aged children by showing (a) that adults still need to inhibit the misleading perceptual strategy – i.e., the direct comparison of the subordinate classes – to reason about class inclusion and (b) that the efficiency of the inhibitory control needed in this specific task increases with age.

Finally, one study to date has used a negative priming paradigm to demonstrate that inhibition is required in syllogistic reasoning (Moutier et al., 2006). As in

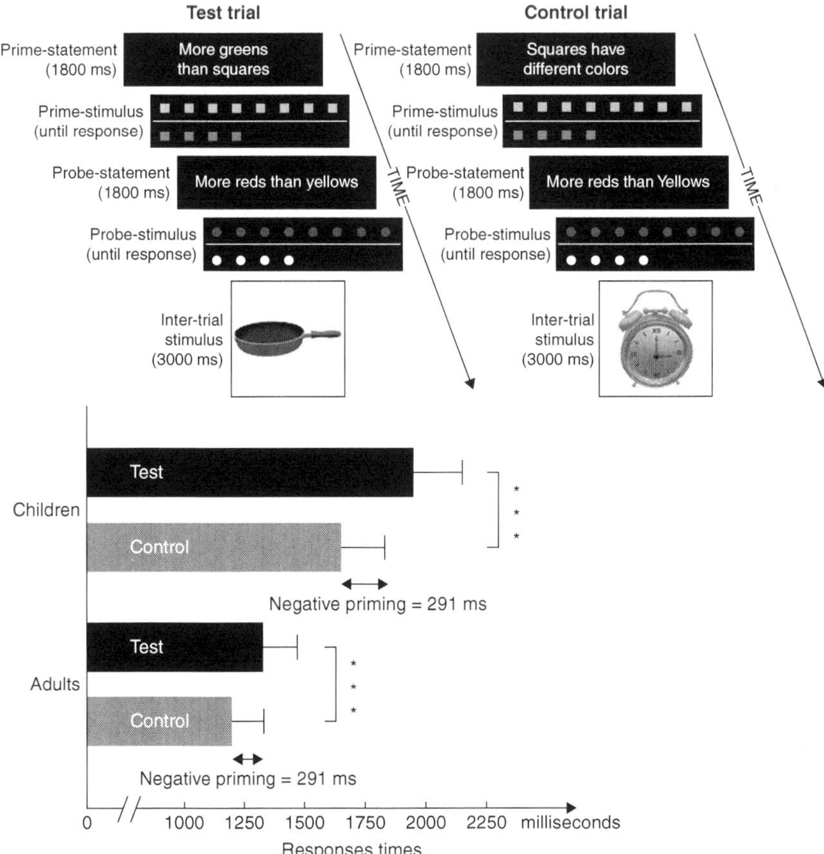

Figure 4.2 Procedures used on test and control trials in the negative priming adaptation of the class-inclusion task (top). Response times in ms on test and control trials in children and adults (bottom). Error bars denote 95% confidence intervals (*** $p < .0005$). Adapted from Borst et al., 2013.

other negative priming studies, children performed test and control trials. Each trial consisted of two syllogisms with many words in common. In test trials, on the prime the validity of the syllogism was in contradiction with children's knowledge of the world (e.g., *All elephants are light*). Therefore, children had to inhibit their belief (e.g. elephants are heavy) to correctly judge the logical validity of the conclusion. On the probe, a syllogism was presented in which children's belief was congruent with the logical validity of the conclusion (e.g., *All elephants are light,* when the conclusion was not valid). Critically, the belief that was inhibited on the prime was congruent with the validity of the syllogism on the probe (see Figure 4.3). On control trials, children solved neutral syllogisms in which the conclusion was neither unacceptable nor acceptable regarding the children's beliefs (e.g., *No students in the blue school are interested in sports*) followed, on the probe, by a syllogism in which the belief was congruent with the logical validity of the conclusion. As expected if inhibitory control is needed for syllogistic

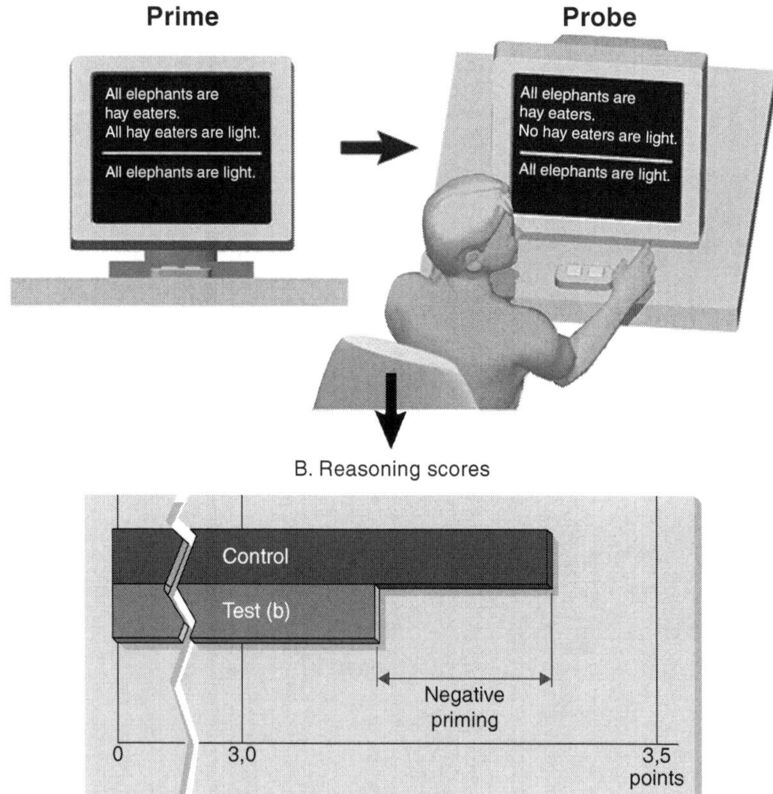

Figure 4.3 Procedure used on test trials in the negative priming adaptation of the syllogistic reasoning task (top). Response times in ms in control and test trials (bottom). Adapted from Moutier et al., 2006.

reasoning, a negative priming effect was reported on the number of errors made by the participants: children committed more errors on the congruent syllogisms (probe items) when performed after syllogisms (prime items) in which beliefs and the validity of the conclusion interfered (see Figure 4.3). Thus, as with the other logicomathematical tasks that we reviewed, syllogistic reasoning seems directly related to the ability to inhibit irrelevant strategies (or beliefs) in order to activate a logical algorithm.

For completeness, recall that in the first section we mentioned the theoretical debate between the selective inhibition and episodic retrieval accounts of negative priming. Note that unlike negative priming of physical stimuli, negative priming of strategy in the reasoning studies that we reviewed cannot be explained by the episodic retrieval account given that the stimuli differ across the primes and the probes. Thus, negative priming of strategies reflects most likely the inhibitory control allowing one to resist to biases, heuristics or beliefs.

Conclusion

A growing body of evidence suggests that one possesses several strategies for solving problems (e.g., Siegler, 1995) and, as the same problem is encountered, one will increasingly rely on an heuristic to solve this problem (e.g., Siegler, 1996, 1999). In some situations, especially conflicting situations, we commit reasoning errors because we tend to rely on those heuristics. Several authors have suggested that inhibition of irrelevant information (heuristics, beliefs, biases) is critical to reason rationally (e.g., Evans, 2003; 2011; Houdé, 2000; 2001; 2007).[2]

In this chapter, we have presented the negative priming methodology that is widely used in the field of selective attention to reveal inhibition processes of physical stimuli. In addition, we hope that this review has made clear that the same methodology can be used in the field of reasoning to study inhibitory control in situation in which heuristics interfere with our logical thinking. Although the underlying process that produces negative priming is still debated, there is no doubt that this methodology constitutes a promising approach to unravel the nature of reasoning errors. Taken together, we believe that the evidence we reviewed here suggests that reasoning errors occur because of inhibition failure rather than because human beings are irrational.

In closing we would like to draw the readers' attention to a wider link with ongoing evolutions in the developmental field and the general research framework of our lab. Over the last three decades, detailed behavioural studies of children's problem solving led to a reconceptualization of cognitive development, from discrete Piagetian stages (see e.g., Piaget, 1984) to one that is analogous to overlapping waves (Siegler, 1999). The latter is in fact consistent with our neo-Piagetian approach of cognitive development, whereby more and less sophisticated solutions compete for expression. In this approach, inhibition of less sophisticated solutions is a critical component of children's conceptual insights associated with more advanced Piagetian stages (Houdé et al., 2000, 2011). Thus, at any point in time, children and adults have potentially available to them heuristics (or intuitions) and logical algorithms. Negative priming, as a hallmark of inhibitory control, reveals the potential cost of blocking our intuitions.

This new approach of cognitive development opens an avenue for designing pedagogical interventions (Diamond et al., 2007; Diamond and Lee, 2011; Houdé, 2007). Inhibition is, indeed, a form of neurocognitive and behavioral control that enables children and adults to resist habits or automatisms, temptations, distractions, or interference, and to adapt to complex reasoning situations by way of mental flexibility.

Notes

1 Critically, the inhibition training included logico-emotional warnings such as

> In this problem, the source of the error lies in a habit we all have of concentrating on items mentioned in the rule and not paying attention to the others. Thus, the goal here is to not fall into the trap. [. . .] Let's consider the different answers and eliminate the wrong answers, which make you fall into the trap.

not present in the logical training.

2 Note that even if this idea is now well accepted in dual-process accounts of reasoning (Evans, 2003, 2011) Houdé (1997b) was the first to introduce inhibition within this theoretical framework in the late 90s (in a commentary on Evans and Over's (1997) paper about Systems 1 and 2 of rationality).

References

Aron, A.R., Robbins, T.W. and Poldrack, R.A. (2004). Inhibition and the right inferior frontal cortex. *Trends in Cognitive Sciences*, *8*, 170–177.

Bartholow, B. D., Pearson, M. A., Dickter, C. L., Sher, K. J., Fabiani, M. and Gratton, G. (2005). Strategic control and medial frontal negativity: Beyond errors and response conflict. *Psychophysiology*, *42*, 33–42.

Borst, G., Pineau, A., Poirel, N., Cassotti, M. & Houdé, O. (2013). Inhibitory control efficiency in a Piaget-like class-inclusion task in school-age children and adults: A developmental negative priming study. *Developmental Psychology*, *49*, 1366–1374.

Dalrymple-Alford, E. C. and Budayr, B. (1966). Examination of some aspects of the Stroop color-word test. *Perceptual and Motor Skills*, *23*, 1211–1214.

Daurignac, E., Houdé, O. and Jouvent, R. (2006). Negative priming in a numerical Piaget-like task in adults as evidenced by ERP. *Journal of Cognitive Neuroscience*, *18*, 730–736.

De Neys, W., Vartanian, O. and Goel, V. (2008). Smarter than we think: When our brains detect that we are biased. *Psychological Science*, *19*, 483–489.

DeSchepper, B. G. and Treisman, A. M. (1991, November). *Novel visual shapes in negative priming*. Paper presented at the 32nd annual meeting of the Psychonomic Society, San Francisco.

Diamond, A. et al. (2007). Preschool program improves cognitive control. *Science*, *318*, 1387–1388.

Diamond, A. and Lee, K. (2011). Interventions shown to aid executive function development in children 4 to 12 years old. *Science*, *333*, 959–964.

Donchin, E., Karis, E., Bashore, T., Coles, M. and Gratton, G. (1986). Cognitive psychophysiology and human information processing. In M. Coles, E. Donchin and S. Porges

(Eds.), *Psychophysiology: Systems, Processes, and Applications* (pp. 244–267). New York: The Guilford Press.

Driver, J. and Tipper, S. P. (1989). On the nonselectivity of selective seeing: Contrasts between interference and priming in selective attention. *Journal of Experimental Psychology: Human Perception and Performance*, *15*, 304–414.

Egner, T. and Hirsch, J. (2005). Where memory meets attention: neural substrates of negative priming. *Journal of Cognitive Neuroscience*, *17*, 1774–1784.

Epstein, S. (1994). Integration of the cognitive and psychodynamic unconscious. *American Psychologists*, *49*, 709–724.

Evans, J. S. B. T. (1972). Reasoning with negatives. *British Journal of Psychology*, *63*, 213–219.

Evans, J. S. B. T. (1989). *Biases in Human Reasoning*. Erlbaum, Hove, UK.

Evans, J. S. B. T. (1998). Matching bias in conditional reasoning. *Thinking Reasoning*,*4*, 45–82.

Evans, J. S. B. T. (2003). In two minds: Dual-process accounts of reasoning. *Trends in Cognitive Sciences*, *7*, 10, 454–459.

Evans, J. S. B. T. (2011). Dual-process theories of reasoning: Contemporary issues and developmental applications. *Developmental Review*, *31*, 86–102.

Evans, J. S. B. T. and Over, D. E. (1997). Rationality in reasoning: The problem of deductive competence. *Current Psychology of Cognition*, *18*, 3–38.

Fox, E. (1995). Negative priming from ignored distractors in visual selection: A review. *Psychonomic Bulletin and Review*, *2*, 145–173.

Frings, C. and Groh-Bordin, C. (2007). Electrophysiological correlates of visual identity negative priming. *Brain Research*, *1176*, 82–91.

Gibbons, H. (2006). An event-related potential investigation of varieties of negative priming. *Journal of Psychophysiology*, *20*, 170–185.

Goel, V., Gold, B., Kapur, S., and Houle, S. (1997). The seats of reason? An imaging study of deductive and inductive reasoning. *NeuroReport*, *8*, 1305–1310.

Goel, V., Gold, B., Kapur, S. and Houle, S. (1998). Neuroanatomical correlates of human reasoning. *Journal of Cognitive Neuroscience*, *10*, 293–302.

Groh-Bordin, C. and Frings, C. (2009). Where has all the inhibition gone? Insights from electrophysiological measures into negative priming without probe distractors. *Brain and Cognition*, *71*, 92–98.

Hinojosa, J. A., Pozo, M. A., Méndez-Bértolo, C. and Luna, D. (2009). Event-related potential correlates of visual identity negative priming unbiased by trial-by-trial effects. *Brain and Cognition*, *69*, 531–537.

Houdé, O. (1997a). Numerical development: From the infant to the child. Wynn's (1992) paradigm in 2- and 3-year-olds. *Cognitive Development*, *12*, 373–392.

Houdé, O. (1997b). Rationality in reasoning: The problem of deductive competence and the inhibitory control of cognition. *Current Psychology of Cognition*, *16*, 108–113.

Houdé, O. (2000). Inhibition and cognitive development: Object, number, categorization, and reasoning. *Cognitive Development*, *15*, 63–73.

Houdé, O. (2007). First insights on "neuropedagogy of reasoning". *Thinking and Reasoning*, *13*, 81–89.

Houdé, O. (2001). Interference and inhibition (psychology of -). In N. J. Smelser and P. B. Baltes (Eds.), *International Encyclopedia of the Social and Behavioral Sciences* (pp. 7718–7722). Oxford: Elsevier Science.

Houdé, O. and Guichart, E. (2001). Negative priming effect after inhibition of number/length interference in a Piaget-like task. *Developmental Science*, *4*, 119–123.

Houdé, O. and Moutier, S. (1996). Deductive reasoning and experimental inhibition training: The case of the matching bias. *Current Psychology of Cognition, 15*, 409–434.

Houdé, O. and Moutier, S. (1999). Deductive reasoning and experimental inhibition training: The case of the matching bias. New data and reply to Girotto. *Current Psychology of Cognition, 18*, 75–85.

Houdé, O., Pineau, A., Leroux, G., Poirel, N., Perchey, G., Lanoë, C., Lubin, A., et al. (2011). Functional MRI study of Piaget's conservation-of-number task in preschool and school-age children: A neo-Piagetian approach. *Journal of Experimental Child Psychology, 110*, 332–346.

Houdé, O., Rossi, S., Lubin, A. and Joliot, M. (2010) Mapping numerical processing, reading, and executive functions in the developing brain: An fMRI meta-analysis of 52 studies including 842 children. *Developmental Science, 13*, 876–885.

Houdé, O., Zago, L., Crivello, F., Moutier, S., Pineau, A., Mazoyer, B. and Tzourio-Mazoyer, N. (2001). Access to deductive logic depends on a right ventromedial prefrontal area devoted to emotion and feeling: evidence from a training paradigm. *NeuroImage, 14*, 1486–1492.

Houdé, O., Zago, L., Mellet, E., Moutier, S., Pineau, A., Mazoyer, B. and Tzourio-Mazoyer, N. (2000). Shifting from the perceptual brain to the logical brain: The neural impact of cognitive inhibition training. *Journal of Cognitive Neuroscience, 12*, 721–728.

Houghton, G. and Tipper, S. P. (1994). A model of inhibitory mechanisms in selective attention.In D. Dagenbach and T. Carr (Eds.), *Inhibitory Mechanisms in Attention, Memory and Language* (pp. 53–112). San Diego, CA: Academic Press.

Houghton, G., Tipper, S. P., Weaver, B. and Shore, D. I. (1996). Inhibition and interference in selective attention: Some tests of a neural network model. *Visual Cognition, 3*, 119–164.

Inhelder, B. and Piaget, J. (1964). *The Early Growth of Logic in the Child.* New York: Routledge and Kegan (original in French, 1959).

Kahneman, D. and Frederick, S. (2002). Representativeness revisited: Attribute substitution in intuitive judgement. In T. Gilovich, D. Griffin and D. Kahneman (Eds.), *Heuristics and Biases: The Psychology of Intuitive Judgement* (pp. 49–81).

Kane, M. J., Hasher, L., Stoltzfus, E. R., Zachs, R. T. and Connelly, S. L. (1994). Inhibitory attentional mechanisms and aging. *Psychology and Aging, 9*, 103–102.

Kathmann, N., Bogdahn, B. and Endrass, T. (2006). Event-related variations during location and identity negative priming. *Neuroscience Letters, 394*, 53–56.

Klauer, K.C., Musch, J. and Naumer, B. (2000). On belief bias in syllogistic reasoning. *Psychological Review, 107*, 852–884.

Krueger, F., Fischer, R., Heinecke, A. and Hagendorf, H. (2007). An fMRI investigation into the neural mechanisms of spatial attentional selection in a location-based negative priming task. *Brain Research, 1174*, 110–119.

Milliken, B., Joordens, S., Merikle, P. A. and Seiffert, A. E. (1998). Selective attention: A reevaluation of the implications of negative priming. *Psychological Review, 105*, 203–229.

Moutier, S. and Houdé, O. (2003). Judgement under uncertainty and conjunction fallacy inhibition training. *Thinking and Reasoning, 9*, 185–201.

Moutier, S., Plagne, S., Melot, A.-M. and Houdé, O. (2006). Syllogistic reasoning and belief-bias inhibition in school children. *Developmental Science, 9*, 166–172.

Neely, J. H. (1977). Semantic priming and retrieval from semantic memory: Role of inhibition-less spreading activation and limited-capacity attention. *Journal of Experimental Psychology: General, 196*, 227–234.

Neill, W. T. (1977). Inhibitory and facilitatory processes in selective attention. *Journal of Experimental Psychology: Human Perception and Performance*, *3*, 444–450.

Neill, W. T. (1979). Switching attention within and between categories: Evidence for intra-category inhibition. *Memory and Cognition*, *7*, 283–290.

Neill, W. T. (1997). Episodic retrieval in negative priming and repetition priming. *Journal of Experimental Psychology: Learning, Memory and Cognition*, *6*, 1291–1305.

Neill, W. T., Lissner, L. S. and Beck, J. L. (1990). Negative priming in *same – different* matching: Further evidence for a central locus of inhibition. *Perception and Psychophysics*, *48*, 398–400.

Neill, W. T. and Valdes, L. A. (1992). Persistence of negative priming: Steady state or decay? *Journal of Experimental Psychology: Learning, Memory and Cognition*, *18*, 565–576.

Neill, W. T., Valdes, L. A. and Terry, K. M. (1992, November). *Negative priming in target localization*. Paper presented at the 33rd annual meeting of the Psychonomic Society, St. Louis.

Neill, W. T., Valdes, L. A. and Terry, K. M. (1995). Selective attention and inhibitory control of cognition. In F. N. Dempster and C. J. Brainerd (Eds.), *Interference and Inhibition in Cognition* (pp. 207–261). New York: Academic Press.

Nieuwenhuis, S., Yeung, N., van den Wildenberg, W. and Ridderinkhof, K. R. (2003). Electrophysiological correlates of anterior cingulated function in a go/no-go task: Effects of response conflict and trial type frequency. *Cognitive, Affective and Behavioral Neuroscience*, *3*, 17–26.

Nyberg, L. (1998) Mapping episodic memory. *Behavioral and Brain Research*, *90*, 107–114.

Park, J. and Kanwisher, N. (1994). Negative priming for spatial locations: Identity mismatching, not distractor inhibition. *Journal of Experimental Psychology: Human Perception and Performance*, *20*, 613–623.

Perret, P., Paour, J.-L. and Blaye, A. (2003). Respective contribution of inhibition and knowledge levels in class inclusion development: A negative priming study. *Developmental Science*, *6*, 283–286.

Piaget, J. (1952). *The Child's Conception of Number*. London: Routledge and Kegan (original in French, Piaget, J. and Szeminska, A., 1941).

Piaget, J. (1984). Piaget's theory. In *Handbook of Child Psychology* (P. H. Mussen, Ed.), Vol. 1, pp. 103–128. Wiley, New York.

Polich, J. and Kok, A. (1995). Cognitive and biological determinants of P300: An integrative review. *Biological Psychology*, *41*, 103–146.

Ruge, H. and Nauman, E. (2006). Brain-electrical correlates of negative location priming under sustained and transient attentional context conditions. *Journal of Psychophysiology*, *20*, 160–169.

Siegler, R.S. (1995). How does change occur: A microgenetic study of number conservation. *Cognitive Psychology*, *25*, 225–273.

Siegler, R.S. (1996). *Emerging Minds: The Process of Change in Children's Thinking*. New York: Oxford University Press.

Siegler, R.S. (1999). Strategic development. *Trends in Cognitive Sciences*, *3*, 430–435.

Steel, C., Haworth, E. J., Peters, E., Hemsley, D. R., Sharma, T., Gray, J. A., Pickering, A., at al. (2001). Neuroimaging correlates of negative priming. *NeuroReport*, *12*, 3619–3624.

Steegen, S. and De Neys, W. (2012). Belief inhibition in children's reasoning: Memory-based evidence. *Journal of Experimental Child Psychology*, *112*, 231–242.

Stroop, J. R. (1935). Studies of interference in serial verbal reactions. *Journal of Experimental Psychology*, *18*, 643–662.

Tipper, S. P. (1985). The negative priming effect: Inhibitory priming by ignored objects. *Quarterly Journal of Experimental Psychology, 37A,* 571–590.

Tipper, S. P. (2001). Does negative priming reflect inhibitory mechanisms? A review and integration of conflicting views. *Quarterly Journal of Experimental Psychology, 54A,* 321–343.

Tipper, S. P. and Cranston, M. (1985). Selective attention and priming: Inhibitory and facilitatory effects of ignored primes. *The Quarterly Journal of Experimental Psychology, 37* (4), 591–611.

Tipper, S. P. and Driver, J. (1988). Negative priming between pictures and words in a selective attention task: Evidence for semantic processing of ignored stimuli. *Memory and Cognition, 16* (1), 64–70.

Tipper, S. P., Brehaut, J. C. and Driver, J. (1990). Selection of moving and static objects for the control of spatially directed action. *Journal of Experimental Psychology: Human Perception and Performance, 16,* 492–504.

Wason, P.C. (1968). Reasoning about a rule. *Quarterly Journal of Experimental Psychology, 60,* 273–281.

Wright, C. I., Keuthen, N. J., Savage, C. R., Martis, B., Williams, D., Wedig, M., McMullin, et al. (2006). Brain correlates of negative and positive visuospatial priming in adults. *NeuroImage, 30,* 983–991.

5 Eye-tracking and reasoning

What your eyes tell about your inferences

Linden J. Ball

Introduction

Human reasoning is fallible when judged against normative standards, such as the conventions of logic. Although people are sometimes capable of impressive acts of inferential analysis, they more often appear to be biased by their intuitions, preconceptions and prior beliefs in ways that lead to reasoning failures (e.g., Evans, 1989; Pohl, 2004). One quintessential example is the pervasive phenomenon of *belief bias*, whereby people tend to endorse the conclusion of an argument on the basis of the conclusion's believability rather than its validity (Evans, Barston and Pollard, 1983). For example, the conclusion to the following syllogistic argument studied by De Neys and Franssens (2009) is logically invalid, yet people tend to endorse it because of its believability: 'All flowers need water. Roses need water. Therefore, roses are flowers'. Belief bias, like all reasoning biases, is remarkably deep-seated and arises even when people are instructed to make only logically necessary inferences and ignore their beliefs.

The present chapter is centrally concerned with efforts to understand the basis of persistent reasoning biases such as belief bias. From a methodological perspective researchers have often been drawn to the use of innovative investigative techniques in an attempt to obtain a theoretical understanding of such biases. Again taking belief bias as an example, in their pioneering research on this phenomenon, Evans et al. (1983) not only established what has since become the standard belief-bias paradigm, which aimed to control for materials confounds that had thwarted previous studies, but they also took the resourceful step of using 'think-aloud' protocol analysis as part of their research methodology. This allowed them to gain important insights into the different premise-driven versus conclusion-driven approaches that people evoke when processing belief-oriented syllogisms, thereby underscoring the crucial involvement of 'strategies' in human reasoning, which has subsequently emerged as a dominant theme in contemporary reasoning research (e.g., Schaeken, De Voogt, Vandierendonck and d'Ydewalle, 1999).

My primary purpose in this chapter is to explicate how data obtained from another innovative technique, that is, eye-tracking, have informed an understanding of reasoning biases. I have long been an enthusiast of the use of eye-movement monitoring in studying reasoning processes, since I believe that the technique can provide a unique window into the moment-by-moment attentional shifts that underlie cognitive performance with multifaceted, display-based problems such as those that are typically presented to participants in reasoning studies. My own interest in eye-tracking studies of reasoning has led to my involvement in the examination of two major reasoning biases. First, I have used the technique to examine the non-logical 'matching' tendencies that dominate responding in abstract versions of Wason's famous four-card selection task (Wason, 1966), which assesses people's abilities at hypothetico-deductive reasoning (e.g., Ball, Lucas, Miles and Gale, 2003). Below I will touch upon some aspects of this research as a way both to introduce the eye-tracking methodology and to explicate the kinds of data that it can provide than can be useful in testing theory-based predictions. Second, I have used eye-tracking to examine belief biases of the type described earlier that arise when people tackle syllogistic arguments that involve categorical terms such as 'all', 'no', 'some' and 'some . . . not' (e.g., Ball, Phillips, Wade and Quayle, 2006). I will discuss eye-tracking studies of belief bias in later sections of this chapter.

One point that is worth stressing early on is that eye-tracking studies of reasoning remain scarce, which means that in this chapter I will sometimes depart from the eye-tracking theme toward a broader consideration of how eye-tracking findings may combine with other sources of convergent data to provide a coherent account of reasoning processes. Indeed, examining the plurality of the evidence deriving from different methods is, in my view, a prerequisite for theoretical progress in the reasoning domain, and is an approach that I have long championed (Ball, 2010; Ormerod and Ball, 2007). Accounting for all of the data that have been garnered through the deployment of varied research techniques, including eye-tracking, is, of course, difficult, but I believe that it is incumbent on reasoning researchers to rise to the challenge and embrace the cross-verification of findings in relation to predictions deriving from extant theories. In the specific case of belief bias, for example, the viability of some long-standing models has been questioned by recent observations that stem from eye-tracking analysis as well as other techniques, including response-time analysis (e.g., Stupple and Ball, 2008; Stupple, Ball, Evans and Kamal-Smith, 2011; Thompson, Striemer, Reikoff, Gunter and Campbell, 2003), the assessment of confidence ratings (e.g., De Neys, Cromheeke and Osman, 2011; Quayle and Ball, 2000), the examination of the correlates of autonomic arousal (De Neys, Moyens and Vansteenwegen, 2010; Morsanyi and Handley, 2012) and neuroimaging analysis (e.g., Goel and Dolan, 2003; Luo, Liu, Stupple, Zhang, Xiao, Jia et al., in press).

The chapter begins with a summary of the eye-tracking method, explaining how eye-movements are recorded and analysed so as to provide data concerning what a person is looking at. Following this summary the chapter then addresses the assumptions that underpin the use of eye-tracking analysis in studies of human cognition in general, and in research on reasoning in particular. To illustrate how eye-tracking can illuminate theories of reasoning, I will initially present findings that derive from eye-movement studies of reasoning performance with the Wason selection task, since such findings have been valuable in clarifying the influence of logical and non-logical factors in determining responding within this paradigm. I will then discuss the use of eye-tracking analysis in belief-bias research, showing how eye-tracking findings have helped to arbitrate between dominant accounts of this phenomenon. To conclude, I will consider ways in which the eye-tracking methodology might be deployed in future studies to address questions and debates regarding the optimal explanation of the biases that pervade people's reasoning.

The eye-tracking method and its underpinning assumptions

Many different methods have been used to record people's eye movements in order to investigate the nature of visually-based activities such as reading (Duchowski, 2007; Wade and Tatler, 2011). Some historical eye-tracking techniques involved the use of electrodes mounted on the skin around the eye to measure differences in electrical potential that correlated with particular eye movements. Other historical techniques involved using a contact lens to cover the cornea (the transparent, front part of the eye that covers the iris and pupil) and the sclera (the white part of the eye), with the edge of the contact lens containing a metal coil. In this way eye movements could be measured by electromagnetic fluctuations when the coil moved along with the eyes. These pioneering methods are highly invasive, whereas most modern eye-tracking systems simply consist of an infrared camera mounted below a display screen that is linked to a desktop computer running image-processing software. The infrared camera allows for a video image to be recorded of eye features that are produced using the 'corneal-reflection/pupil-centre' method (see below), which enables an accurate measure to be gained of where a person is looking (their 'point-of-regard').

In operation, the corneal-reflection/pupil-centre method (e.g., Goldberg and Wichansky, 2003) involves infrared light from an LED embedded within the camera being directed into the eye to create strong reflections in target eye features (note that infrared light is used to avoid dazzling the participant with visible light). The light enters the retina and much of it is reflected back, making the pupil appear as a bright disc (the 'bright pupil' effect; Figure 5.1). The corneal reflection or 'first Purkinje image' is also generated by the infrared light, appearing as a small, sharp glint (Figure 5.1). Once image processing software has identified the centre of the pupil and the location of the corneal reflection, the vector between them is measured and trigonometric calculations enable point-of-regard to be ascertained with great accuracy. Although it is possible to determine approximate point-of-regard using the corneal reflection alone, the benefit of using the corneal-reflection/pupil-centre approach is that eye movements can be dissociated from head movements (Duchowski, 2007; Jacob and Karn, 2003).

Video-based eye trackers need to be calibrated to a person's individual eye movements. This involves employing a pre-experiment method whereby a participant looks at a series of dots that appear in pre-defined locations, typically forming a nine-point grid-pattern covering the full extent of the screen. For each fixated dot the computer records the pupil-centre/corneal-reflection relationship as corresponding to the specific x, y coordinate of where that dot is positioned on

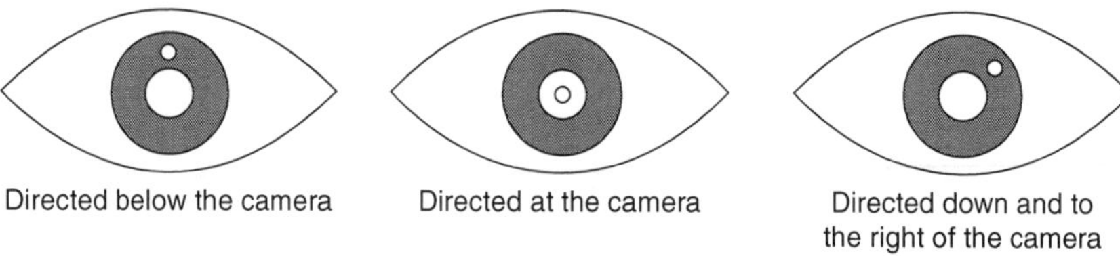

Figure 5.1. Using the corneal-reflection/pupil-centre method to determine point-of-regard when the eye is looking in different directions relative to a camera located in front of the person. Note that light is reflected back from the retina, making the pupil appear as a bright disc at the centre of the eye. The corneal reflection or 'first Purkinje image' appears as a small, sharp glint. The corneal reflection position changes in a measurable way relative to the bright pupil, dependent on the individual's point-of-regard.

the screen. From this calibration process the computer can then interpolate across the screen to determine the x, y coordinates for any point-of-regard.

Two main measures are used as a starting point for further analyses in eye-tracking studies of cognition: fixations and saccades. Fixations are moments when the eyes are relatively stationary so that information at the point-of-regard can be taken in and encoded by the person. Saccades are quick eye movements that occur between fixations, during which visual perception is suppressed to avoid image blurring. There are also numerous metrics that can be derived from fixations and saccades. One important metric in reasoning research is 'gaze', which is a cumulative measure of two or more *continuous* fixations on the same location (see Poole and Ball, 2006, for an overview of eye-movement metrics).

Where a person is fixating is assumed to provide an index of the thought 'on top of the stack' of cognitive processes (Just and Carpenter, 1976). This so-called 'eye-mind' assumption means that eye-movement recordings can be viewed as providing a dynamic trace of where a person's *attention* is being directed when examining information within a visual display. Furthermore, fixation duration and gaze duration are measures that both provide a good index of *ease of processing*, with longer durations indicating greater processing difficulty (Liversedge, Paterson and Pickering, 1998). Interestingly, although it is possible to move attention covertly without moving one's eyes (e.g., looking at one thing but thinking about something else), it is acknowledged that with visually-based stimuli it is far more efficient to move one's eyes *overtly* to the attended information rather than merely to move one's attention (e.g., He and Kowler, 1992; Sclingensiepen, Campbell, Legge and Walker, 1986). Moreover, there is substantial evidence indicating that attention actually *precedes* eye movements to new locations (e.g., Hoffman and Subramaniam, 1995; Kowler, Anderson, Dosher and Blaser, 1995) and that attentional movements and saccades are linked in an obligatory manner (Deubel and Schneider, 1996).

Many readers may find it surprising that people first transfer their attention to a new location, with their eyes then following this covert attention shift. There is, however, good evidence from studies of reading and scene perception that this is, indeed, what typically arises (e.g., Rayner, 1998). It appears that when the processing of the fixated item (e.g., a word or an object) reaches some critical level (e.g., a stage of familiarity or recognition) then the person's attention shifts toward a new item (e.g., the next word in a sentence). This allows for the processing of the new item to commence whilst also signalling the need for the eye-movement system to prepare a motor program to enable a saccade to be made to the item. The time-lag between the attention shift and the execution of the saccade, whilst very brief, allows for low-level visual information to be acquired about the attended item even before it is directly fixated.

In sum, in complex information-processing tasks such as reading or making inferences from visually-presented reasoning problems, the evidence suggests that there is a tight coupling between the location of the eyes and the locus of attentional processing (Rayner, 1998), that is, what people are looking at is what they are thinking about. The validity of the eye-mind assumption is clearly vital for the use of the technique in reasoning research and for the meaningful interpretation of eye-tracking data in relation to reasoning theories.

Illustrative eye-tracking findings: matching bias in the Wason selection task

Researchers have recently started to capitalize on eye-tracking data to examine fundamental processes in thinking, reasoning and problem solving (e.g., Ferguson and Sanford, 2008; Grant and Spivey, 2003; Jones, 2003; Knoblich, Ohlsson and Raney, 2001; Litchfield and Ball, 2011). My own initial efforts at applying eye-tracking analysis in reasoning research concerned examining the processes underlying performance on the Wason selection task (Ball et al., 2003). I elaborate on this research below after first explaining the nature of the selection task and the theoretical ideas that were tested by deploying the eye-tracking technique.

In a traditional *abstract* version of the selection task participants are presented with a rule of the form 'If p then q' and are shown four cards to which the rule refers. For example, the rule might be 'If there is a K on one side of the card then there is a 3 on the other side', with the facing sides of cards showing K, B, 3, and 7, which correspond to the logical values, *p*, *not-p*, *q*, and *not-q*, respectively. Participants are informed that each card has a letter on one side and a number on the other side, and are instructed to decide which card or cards need to be turned over to determine whether the rule is true or false. The logically correct choices for a conditional reading of the rule are K and 7 (*p* and *not-q*), but few participants make these selections, instead choosing K alone (*p*), or else K and 3 (*p* and *q*). Wason's explanation of this selection pattern was that it reflected a 'verification bias' (Wason and Johnson-Laird, 1972), in that people were supposedly attempting to confirm the truth of the rule by finding a card with a supporting K and 3 combination, rather than striving to reveal the potential falsity of the rule – as logic necessitates – by searching for letter-number combinations that would present counterexamples to the rule.

Wason's verification-bias account of the selection task was shown to be incorrect in a study by Evans and Lynch (1973), which permuted negative components through the presented rules, leading to conditionals such as 'If there is an K on one side of the card then there is *not* a 3 on the other side'. What is interesting about such negated rules is that they change the logic of the task and thence the cards that participants should select to determine the rule's truth or falsity. What Evans and Lynch showed, however, was that responses remained largely unchanged, despite the presence of negated items. This observation suggests that participants simply select cards that 'match' the letter and number items named in the rule, irrespective of the presence of negative terms. This *matching bias* phenomenon (Evans, 1989) is highly robust in studies using abstract materials and the negations paradigm (see Evans, 1998, for a meta-analysis).

In terms of theoretical developments, the reliable observation of matching bias in selection task studies was a key factor that led Evans to formulate his general heuristic-analytic (H–A) account of reasoning (e.g., Evans, 1984, 1989). *Heuristic* processes were viewed by Evans as being preconscious, functioning to focus attention selectively on information that appears *relevant* to the task at hand, such as the cards that match the items mentioned in the rule in the selection task. People subsequently reason from these heuristically-driven representations using *analytic* processes that allow for the generation of inferences or judgements. According to the H–A theory, biases in reasoning arise primarily because either logically relevant information is excluded at the heuristic stage or logically irrelevant information is included. In relation to the abstract selection task, the original H–A theory (e.g., Evans, 1984, 1989) proposed that heuristics such as 'matching' determine card choices for the majority of individuals, with analytic processing serving merely to rationalize why these cards seem worthy of selection (for evidence of such rationalization see Evans and Wason, 1976; Lucas and Ball, 2005). In this latter respect, the selection task was viewed by Evans as being different to other reasoning problems, for which analytic processing appears to play at least some role in influencing decisions.

Although Evans' H–A account of reasoning has undergone various revisions over the past decade (e.g., Evans, 2006), it still revolves around a two-stage reasoning process, with heuristics delivering initial 'default' intuitions that may or may not be intervened upon and overridden by subsequent analytic processes. This kind of dual-process architecture has been described as *default-interventionist* by Evans (e.g., 2007; see also Evans and Stanovich, 2013), and provides an explanation for why default intuitions (such as a bias toward matching cards in the selection task) often determine final reasoning responses, since they fail to be overridden by analytic processes, especially in situations where people have to reason in a time-limited manner (e.g., Roberts and Newton, 2011). Furthermore, attributing an interventionist role to analytic processes provides a means by which external factors and person variables can influence reasoning. There is evidence, for example, that reasoning can be facilitated by instructions to reason logically, by dispositions to think critically, and by individual differences in cognitive ability (e.g., Evans and Stanovich, 2013; Stanovich, 2009; Stanovich and West, 1998;

Stanovich, West and Toplak, 2007). A further advantage of the revised H–A theory and its default-interventionist principles is that it allows for biases in reasoning not only to arise at the heuristic stage (e.g., as a result of the dominance of default responses) but also from deficiencies in analytic processing (Evans, 2006). In this latter respect Evans views the analytic stage as being inherently *satisficing* in its operation, seeking reasoning solutions that are 'good enough' in terms of satisfying task goals.

Returning to the abstract selection task, it is noteworthy that Evans' H–A account inspired a particular research methodology that was directed at testing the key tenets of the theory, which involved the analysis of people's *card inspection times*. Evans (1996) argued that if card selections reflect the operation of preconscious heuristics, then people will primarily look at cards that are cued by these heuristics. Furthermore, they will end up selecting these cards once they have rationalized the heuristically-based intuition that these are the right cards to choose. In other words, those cards that are associated with higher selection rates should be associated with longer inspection times, and for any given card, those participants who choose it will demonstrate longer inspection times than those who do not. To test these predictions Evans (1996) implemented a method whereby selection tasks were presented on a computer and participants had to point with a mouse at any card they were 'thinking about', with the computer logging pointing times for each card. The results provided good support for Evans' H–A predictions. For example, there were large and significant differences in the mean inspection times observed for selected versus non-selected cards, with the former generally being greater than 4 seconds and the latter typically less than 2 seconds.

Although the inspection-time technique supported Evans' predictions, there are numerous methodological artifacts associated with the mouse-pointing approach that could have produced spurious support for the H–A theory. For example, Roberts (1998) suggested that people may be inclined to pause the mouse pointer over a card for a brief moment before making an active 'select' decision. Since Evans (1996) only required active responses for selected cards, such momentary hesitations would add additional time to the cumulative inspection-time values for selected versus rejected cards. Yet another example of a problematic task-format bias that Roberts (1998) notes is described as 'sensory leakage', which would arise if cards are being inspected and rejected even before the mouse pointer has had a chance to reach them. This would again tend to add additional time to selected cards, which we know from previous research are decided about earlier than rejected cards (Evans, Ball and Brooks, 1987). Roberts (1998) manipulated the presence of these kinds of task-format biases across a series of imaginative experiments, and showed very clearly that the magnitude of the inspection-time effect was closely related to the number of sources of bias that were present.

The main issue highlighted by Roberts' (1998) critique of the inspection-time paradigm is that mouse-pointing seems to lack sensitivity as a way for participants to reflect their moment-by-moment attentional shifts when processing cards in the selection task. This insensitivity seems to derive from the *indirect* measure of attentional processing that mouse-pointing affords, with participants having to *self-monitor* their attentional focus and *actively* move the pointer from one card to another as their attention shifts. To overcome the problematic artifacts associated with mouse-pointing, Ball et al. (2003) instead used eye-gaze tracking as a far better method to monitor people's card-inspection times. For the reasons explained previously, eye-tracking provides a highly *direct* measure of people's second-by-second attentional shifts. In addition, when combined with careful task constructions (e.g., a requirement for select/reject decisions for all cards in order to standardize the gaze time associated with the act of decision registration), the eye-tracking methodology clearly represents a major advancement in the assessment of people's processing of information within the selection task paradigm.

Ball et al.'s (2003) results provided compelling evidence in support of Evans' H–A predictions, with cumulative gaze on selected cards (which are typically matching items) being reliably greater than on rejected cards (which are typically non-matching items). These longer looking times for selected cards were taken to be a reflection of the time that people spent in confabulating explanations in order to rationalize heuristically-cued choices (cf. Evans, 1996). In some recent follow-up research, however, Evans and Ball (2010) noted a more nuanced possibility, which is that people may reason in a consequential manner in relation to certain heuristically-cued cards, such that they end up changing their intuitive decisions for those items. This is because there are certain matching cards that arise with particular rule forms in the selection task paradigm for which it is very difficult to find a good reason to justify a selection decision. In other words, whilst a person's initial intuition is that the card should be chosen, when they apply subsequent analytic processing they are unable to rationalize the card's selection and instead reject it, thereby breaking the link between longer gaze times and selection decisions.

In a detailed re-analysis of Ball et al.'s (2003) original eye-tracking data, Evans and Ball (2010) showed good support for this new prediction for a dissociation between the selection rates and gaze duration for certain matching cards associated with particular rule forms. Thus, whilst the cards in question were gazed at for as long as other matching cards, they were selected much less frequently. Evans and Ball reached the inescapable conclusion that since people consider such matching cards but then do *not* select them then they must be applying analytic processes that are doing more than merely rationalizing heuristically-cued cards. This evidence is in line with Evans' (2006) revised H–A theory, which argues that analytic processing functions in a satisficing manner, striving for reasonable justifications for either maintaining or overriding intuitive decisions in order to attain task goals.

The preceding foray into the way in which eye-tracking data have been used to examine matching bias in the abstract selection task demonstrates the power of the method to reveal important new findings. For example, the method has arguably provided some of the most compelling evidence to date that analytic reasoning does, after all, play a key role in determining whether heuristically-cued cards are subsequently selected or rejected. This evidence challenges a long-standing assumption of the original H–A theory of the selection task (e.g., Evans, 1984,

1996), but aligns well with Evans' (2006) revised H–A theory. In the next section I move on to consider how eye-tracking has similarly helped to challenge existing ideas regarding the processing of belief-oriented syllogisms.

Informing an understanding of belief bias using eye-tracking

The key findings relating to belief-bias effects in reasoning were established in Evans et al.'s (1983) standard paradigm, which made use of categorical syllogisms. These are deductive arguments that involve two premises and a conclusion, such as: 'All mammals can walk. Whales are mammals. Therefore, whales can walk' (note that this example and the one that follows are from De Neys and Franssens, 2009). *Valid* conclusions describe the relationship between the terms that are presented in the premises in a way that is *necessarily true* (i.e., the presented premises do not give rise to any counterexamples that falsify the given conclusion). The previous syllogism is logically valid, even though it has an unbelievable conclusion. Validity is, therefore, a syntactic construct that does not depend on the actual semantic content of the given premises and conclusions. *Invalid* conclusions are ones that do not necessarily follow from the premises, even though they may be consistent with the premises (i.e., the premises allow for counterexamples to be constructed that contradict the conclusion). So, for example, the following syllogism is invalid despite the conclusion's apparent believability 'All things with an engine need oil. Cars need oil. Therefore, cars have engines'.

What is almost always observed in studies that have used syllogisms to study belief-bias effects is that people display a non-logical tendency to endorse presented conclusions that are compatible with beliefs more frequently than conclusions that contradict beliefs. Importantly, too, this belief-bias effect is more pronounced on invalid than on valid problems, giving rise to a logic by belief interaction in conclusion-endorsement rates. Formulating an effective explanation of this interaction has been a non-trivial endeavour for researchers, with numerous competing theories having been spawned over the last 30 years and with no resolution in sight in relation to the ongoing debate.

One issue that has complicated theorising in this area is that whilst the effects of belief bias on reasoning are both pervasive and fairly impervious to instructional influences there are, nevertheless, factors that sometimes appear to moderate the emergence of the bias. For example, recent findings suggest that belief bias may be less prevalent among reasoners of higher cognitive capacity (e.g., De Neys, 2006; Newstead, Handley, Harley, Wright and Farelly, 2004; Sá, West and Stanovich, 1999), although this evidence seems far from clear-cut (see Pitchford, 2013). Indeed, what seems to be more important than cognitive capacity in ameliorating belief bias is a person's disposition toward engaging in open-minded thinking and inhibiting intuitive responses (e.g., Pitchford, 2013; Sá et al., 1999; Stanovich, 2009, Stanovich and West, 1997; Thompson, Morley and Newstead, 2011). Although, then, a few unique individuals do seem to have some ability or disposition to overcome the biasing effects of beliefs during reasoning, the general picture is that for the majority of reasoners, belief bias is a factor that detracts from normative responding (but see Ball, 2013, for recent evidence that the provision of trial-by-trial evaluative feedback to participants on their reasoning success can be effective in eradicating the bias).

Contemporary models of belief bias are typically couched within a dual-process framework, much along the 'default-interventionist' lines described in relation to the Wason selection task, with the phenomenon being viewed as arising from the interplay between belief-based 'heuristic' processes that are rapid, associative and implicit, and 'analytic' processes that are slow, sequential and explicit. The belief-bias effect suggests that heuristic processes may often dominate responding with certain belief-oriented syllogisms. One such dual-process theory that featured strongly in early belief-bias research is the 'selective scrutiny' model, originally proposed by Evans et al. (1983). This model assumes that believable conclusions are responded to heuristically (i.e., they are simply accepted), whereas unbelievable conclusions motivate more rigorous analytic processing directed at testing conclusion validity. This model thereby explains the logic by belief interaction as arising from the more assiduous scrutiny that is directed at syllogisms with unbelievable conclusions.

A similar model that also focuses on the idea that unbelievable conclusions elicit an analytic reasoning strategy is captured within the mental models theory of belief bias forwarded by Oakhill and Johnson-Laird (1985; Oakhill, Johnson-Laird and Garnham, 1989). According to this account, conclusions that are supported by people's initial 'mental models' of the given premises will simply be accepted if they are believable, but if a conclusion is unbelievable then it will be tested more carefully against alternative and potentially falsifying mental models of the premises (i.e., unbelievable conclusions can be viewed as triggering a disconfirmatory or 'selective falsification' strategy). In this way, the occurrence of a logic by belief interaction can be explained, since believable conclusions will tend to be endorsed, whereas unbelievable conclusions may either be endorsed or rejected, dependent on the outcome of the more diligent process of counterexample search, which will establish their validity or invalidity.

Both the mental models account and the older, selective scrutiny account allow for the derivation of inspection-time predictions that can readily be tested via eye-tracking analysis. For example, reasoners should inspect the premises of problems with unbelievable conclusions longer than the premises of problems with believable conclusions. This is because they will be more likely to seek out counterexample models in the former case, which would necessitate premise re-reading to refresh and revise the mental representation of the information that the premises contain. A more detailed inspection-time prediction is also possible in relation to the temporal locus of the expected inspection-time effect, that is, it should occur *after* a conclusion has been inspected, because the increased processing that people are claimed to engage in for problems with unbelievable conclusions is directly contingent on the believability status of the conclusion.

Ball et al. (2006) set out to use eye-tracking to test the predictions deriving from the selective scrutiny and mental models accounts of belief bias. The upshot was very revealing. Bear in mind that both theories predict longer inspection times for the premises of *unbelievable* conclusions. The results indicated the exact opposite, with inspection times being longer for the premises of *believable* conclusions (Table 5.1; see also Thompson et al., 2003, for similar evidence from response latencies). Ball et al.'s (2006) eye-tracking study also revealed the existence of a reliable interaction between logic and belief in both a local measure of premise inspection times and in a global measure of overall syllogism processing times. The interaction indicated that people spent longer reasoning about the 'conflict' syllogisms, where conclusion validity and believability are in competition (i.e., those with invalid-believable conclusions and valid-unbelievable conclusions) relative to the 'non-conflict' syllogisms, where conclusion validity and believability concur (i.e., those with valid-believable and invalid-unbelievable conclusions). A final, intriguing result was that the logic by belief interaction as measured in relation to premise inspection times was localised at a post-conclusion-viewing stage (i.e., the effect only arose *after* participants had read the conclusion and processed its belief status; see Table 5.1). This latter finding suggests that in some crucial respect people's reasoning is selectively guided by the believability of the given conclusion, but that this happens in a manner unlike that predicted by the selective scrutiny and mental models theories.

The interaction between logic and belief observed in Ball et al.'s (2006) eye-tracking experiment has been replicated in recent studies using computer-based tracking techniques to log the processing times for syllogism components – but without recourse to eye-movement monitoring (e.g., Stupple and Ball, 2008). There now appears to be consistent evidence that conflict problems take longer to process than non-conflict problems, which Stupple and Ball (2008) have taken to indicate that participants are in some sense *aware* that the logic of a conclusion and its belief status are in opposition, such that extra processing effort has to be allocated to resolving the conflict. Stupple and Ball further suggest that these ideas align most closely with a 'parallel-process' model of belief bias in which heuristic and analytic processes operate *simultaneously* to generate a response, with conflicts arising whenever different responses are produced by the two processing streams (cf. Sloman, 2002). Presumably, too, because of the uncertainty that is

Table 5.1 Mean inspection times (in seconds) for premises, conclusions, and overall, as a function of conclusion validity and conclusion believability, as reported by Ball et al. (2006).

	Believable		*Unbelievable*	
	Valid	Invalid	Valid	Invalid
Premises: Pre-conclusion	4.27	4.27	4.12	4.03
Premises: Post-conclusion	6.36	9.71	7.21	5.56
Premises: Total	10.62	13.97	11.33	9.57
Conclusion	4.37	6.14	4.00	3.97
Overall	14.99	20.11	15.32	13.54

Note: *Pre-conclusion* denotes the time spent inspecting the premises prior to the first fixation upon the conclusion, and *Post-conclusion* denotes the time spent inspecting the premises after the first fixation upon the conclusion.

engendered by entering a state of heuristic/analytic conflict there will also be a tendency for people to default to a heuristic response as a form of 'computational-escape hatch' in order to avoid applying further processing effort (cf. Ball and Quayle, 2000; Stanovich and West, 2000). This latter notion has resonances with the 'metacognitive uncertainty' account of belief bias proposed by Quayle and Ball (2000), in which belief-based responding is viewed as arising *after* a failed attempt at a logical analysis of a conclusion's validity or invalidity.

Recently, De Neys (2012) has proposed a novel dual-process model of belief bias that embodies both parallel and sequential processing components. The model also aims to capture the finding noted above that people appear to have some *awareness* of logic/belief conflicts, as revealed through their subjective confidence judgements (e.g., Quayle and Ball, 2000) and measurements of autonomic arousal (e.g., De Neys, Moyens and Vansteenwegen, 2010). The arousal data are particularly compelling in revealing that people have an implicit awareness that the heuristic responses that they tend to make to conflict items are, in fact, normatively incorrect (cf. Morsanyi and Handley, 2012). De Neys suggests that people's indirect sensitivity to the normative status of presented conflict conclusions is indicative of their possession of an 'intuitive logic' that can be applied rapidly, implicitly and in parallel to a stream of intuitive, implicit heuristic processing. Thus, logic/belief conflicts are viewed by De Neys as arising from two kinds of processes that function at a purely intuitive level. Any deliberative conclusion analysis that arises for belief-oriented syllogisms is viewed as being evoked as a consequence of a reasoner's awareness of an intuition-based conflict, with such deliberation thence being applied in an attempt to resolve the conflict.

De Neys' (2012) 'logical intuition model' represents a radical departure from other dual-process models in the literature, yet has considerable appeal in terms of providing a hybrid approach in which *intuitive heuristic* and *intuitive logical* processes that operate in parallel can subsequently have their outputs scrutinized by analytic processes. It will be interesting to see whether further research using a full range of methodologies lends support to the novel idea that both logical and heuristic processes can function at an implicit level.

Future directions for eye-tracking studies of reasoning

In this chapter I have illustrated how dual-process theories of reasoning have benefited from insights arising from the deployment of eye-tracking technology to study people's gaze times on task components when they tackle presented problems. In the case of the selection task, for example, Evans and Ball's (2010) re-analysis of eye-tracking data obtained by Ball et al. (2003) provide striking evidence that heuristic processes are not solely responsible for card selections. Rather, the evidence indicates that analytic processes *do* play a causal role in determining whether heuristically-cued cards are subsequently selected or rejected. Such findings reveal how eye-tracking data can provide unique results that challenge established conceptual models and thereby advance theorising in important ways. The fact that analytic processing plays more than a purely rationalizing role in reasoning is clearly of critical relevance to understanding the nature of higher cognition in humans and its importance in achieving task-specific goals. Furthermore, the evidence for analytic processing being correlated with normative responding is reassuring as a counterpoint to the view that we are ruled, for better or worse, by our intuitions (e.g., Gladwell, 2005).

It is noteworthy that over the past few years research on the selection task, whether in its abstract or thematic variants, has largely gone out of fashion, even though there is no doubt much still to understand about the reasoning processes that the task evokes, which could be addressed through further eye-tracking studies (see Ball, Lucas and Phillips, 2005, for eye-tracking studies of deontic selection tasks). Nevertheless, there are good reasons for why reasoning researchers have moved away from being hide-bound by artificial paradigms such as the selection task, not least the desire to understand the nature of reasoning that arises in everyday, informal contexts (e.g., Hornikx and Hahn, 2012).

In contrast to the selection task, research using the belief-bias paradigm is currently flourishing, perhaps because it comes closer to capturing everyday aspects of informal argumentation (but see Thompson and Evans, 2012). As I have outlined, eye-tracking and response-time studies with belief-oriented reasoning problems (e.g., Ball et al., 2006; Thompson et al., 2003) have served to undermine long-standing accounts of the belief-bias effect. For example, both the selective scrutiny and mental models accounts predict that problems with unbelievable conclusions should be processed more rigorously than those with believable conclusions, yet eye-tracking and response-time data consistently reveal the opposite finding.

In addition, the eye-tracking data discussed previously not only show that problems with *believable* conclusions are processed more assiduously than those with unbelievable conclusions, but that the effect of believability on processing times is itself modulated by conclusion validity. This modulating effect of validity on conclusion believability has proved to be a particularly important finding. The most recent evidence has, in fact, clarified that reliably extended processing times are restricted to the *invalid-believable* conflict items rather than arising with both types of conflict items (Stupple et al., 2011, Thompson et al. 2011). Moreover, individual differences analyses examining processing times as a function of reasoning ability have indicated that the increased processing arising with invalid-believable items is especially pronounced for more cognitively able reasoners (Stupple et al., 2011, Thompson et al. 2011). Invalid-believable syllogisms are notoriously difficult, since people are biased toward conclusion acceptance because of the believable nature of the conclusion and the fact that initial mental models seem to confirm conclusion validity. It is perhaps not so surprising, then, that it is only the most able reasoners who have the ability to resist the endorsement of such conclusions in favour of searching more rigorously for possible counterexample models of the premises, which can be discovered, although this clearly takes time and effort.

I also note here that De Neys' (2012) logical intuition model may well be able to capture these cognitive ability effects that arise in belief-bias research, since although all reasoners appear to detect logic/beliefs conflict at an intuitive level, it is only those of high ability who seem to be able to apply their analytic skills to make normatively appropriate decisions. Although Thompson et al. (2011) favour other, more established theories of belief bias rather than De Neys' logical intuition model, further empirical work is evidently needed to arbitrate between these alternative accounts. Eye-tracking data are likely to be informative in this endeavour, especially when combined with an individual differences approach that focuses on cognitive variables (e.g., working memory capacity) and dispositional factors, such as people's prosperity to engage in a motivated attempt at analytic processing (e.g., Stanovich, 2009).

It is noteworthy that a key strength of eye-tracking analyses in the context of reasoning research is its non-invasive nature. People only need to sit reasonably still whilst processing visually-presented problems unencumbered by restrictive apparatus. The technology produces a fairly pure measure of attentional processing, which can be taken to index the current locus of reasoning. Eye-tracking seems set to be used more frequently in on-going studies of reasoning across a multiplicity of tasks and paradigms, particularly given the inexpensive nature of the equipment and the ease of data collection and analysis. One area of eye-tracking research in the reasoning domain that is currently burgeoning concerns the analysis of eye-movement metrics directly linked to participants' comprehension of visually presented logical statements. A good example of recent research of this type comes from Stewart, Haigh and Ferguson (2013), who used eye-tracking to examine how readers process 'if . . . then' statements used to communicate conditional speech acts such as tips and promises. Conditional promises require that the speaker has control over the outcome event, whereas conditional tips do not necessitate such a requirement. A number of eye-tracking measures revealed that conditional promises that violated expectations regarding the presence of speaker control resulted in processing disruption, whereas conditional tips were processed equally easily regardless whether speaker control was present or absent. Stewart et al. conclude that readers rapidly utilize pragmatic information related to perceived control in order to represent conditional speech acts as they are read.

On-line studies of reasoning of this latter type that examine 'reasoning as we read' seem likely to open up many new possibilities for advancing an understanding of reasoning processes. All forms of propositional statements seem readily amenable to such eye-tracking analyses, whereby some aspect of the presented content or context can be manipulated, such as the probabilities associated with the various components of causal and counterfactual conditionals (e.g., see work by Haigh, Stewart and Connell, 2013, that has used reading-time measures rather than eye-tracking analysis). These kinds of analyses are likely to contribute toward a deeper understanding of reasoning processes, especially by providing converging data that can enable arbitration between competing accounts.

In terms of even more ambitious ideas for future eye-tracking research on reasoning, one area of likely interest concerns whether we can use an individual reasoner's eye-movement patterns in a prognostic manner so as to make accurate predictions about how they will reason on other tasks. For example, if someone is categorized via their eye-movement data as being a conclusion-driven reasoner with, say, belief-oriented syllogisms, how likely is it that this categorization will be predictive of them deploying a conclusion-driven reasoning strategy on tasks involving abstract syllogisms or requiring transitive inference or relational reasoning? Evidence concerning the consistency and generality of reasoning strategies and the manner in which such strategies correlate with other measures of ability could allow researchers to get to the heart of some key issues relating to individual differences in reasoning that could usefully inform theoretical debates.

In conclusion, it seems certain that eye-tracking studies of reasoning will become a key methodology in the future that will run alongside the traditional experimental analysis of responses as well as a whole host of other techniques such as confidence ratings, neuroimaging and the monitoring of autonomic arousal. The resulting data triangulation will provide the richest picture yet of the reasoning processes that mediate between initial problem representations and final response generation.

Acknowledgements

I am grateful to the following collaborators for many valuable exchanges regarding the nature of reasoning processes: Erin Beatty, Jonathan Evans, Maggie Gale, Damien Litchfield, Erica Lucas, Tom Ormerod, Melanie Pitchford, Ed Stupple, Valerie Thompson and Meredith Wilkinson. I also thank Wim De Neys and Magda Osman for undertaking very thorough critical readings of earlier versions of this chapter and for providing valuable feedback that has greatly improved the readability and coherence of this contribution.

References

Ball, L. J. (2010). The dynamics of reasoning: Chronometric analysis and dual-process theories. In K. I. Manktelow, D. E. Over and S. Elqayam (Eds.), *The Science of Reason: A Festschrift for Jonathan S. B. T Evans* (pp. 283–307). Hove, UK: Psychology Press.

Ball, L. J. (2013). Microgenetic evidence for the beneficial effects of feedback and practice on belief bias. *Journal of Cognitive Psychology*, *25*, 183–191.

Ball, L. J., Lucas, E. J., Miles, J. N. V. and Gale, A.G. (2003). Inspection times and the selection task: What do eye-movements reveal about relevance effects? *Quarterly Journal of Experimental Psychology*, *56A*, 1053–1077.

Ball, L. J., Lucas, E. J. and Phillips, P. (2005). Eye movements and reasoning: Evidence for relevance effects and rationalisation processes in deontic selection tasks. In B. G. Bara, L. Barsalou and M. Bucciarelli (Eds.), *Proceedings of the Twenty-Seventh Annual Conference of the Cognitive Science Society* (pp. 196–201). Alpha, NJ: Sheridan Printing.

Ball, L. J., Phillips, P., Wade, C. N. and Quayle, J. D. (2006). Effects of belief and logic on syllogistic reasoning: Eye-movement evidence for selective processing models. *Experimental Psychology*, *53*, 77–86.

Ball, L. J. and Quayle, J. D. (2000). Alternative task construals, computational escape hatches, and dual-system theories of reasoning [Commentary]. *Behavioral and Brain Sciences*, *23*, 667.

De Neys, W. (2006). Dual processing in reasoning: Two systems but one reasoner. *Psychological Science, 17*, 428–433.

De Neys, W. (2012). Bias and conflict: A case for logical intuitions. *Perspectives on Psychological Science, 7*, 28–38.

De Neys, W., Cromheeke, S. and Osman, M. (2011). Biased but in doubt: Conflict and decision confidence. *PLoS ONE, 6*, e15954.

De Neys, W. and Franssens, S. (2009). Belief inhibition during thinking: Not always winning but at least taking part. *Cognition, 113*, 45–61.

De Neys, W., Moyens, E. and Vansteenwegen, D. (2010). Feeling we're biased: Autonomic arousal and reasoning conflict. *Cognitive, Affective, and Behavioral Neuroscience, 10*, 208–216.

Deubel, H. and Schneider, W. X. (1996). Saccade target selection and object recognition: Evidence for a common attentional mechanism. *Vision Research, 36*, 1827–1837.

Duchowski, A. T. (2007). *Eye Tracking Methodology: Theory and Practice, Second Edition.* London, UK: Springer.

Evans, J. S. B. T. (1984). Heuristic and analytic processes in reasoning. *British Journal of Psychology*, 75, 451–468.

Evans, J. S. B. T. (1989). *Bias in Human Reasoning: Causes and Consequences*. Hove, UK: Erlbaum.

Evans, J. S. B. T. (1996). Deciding before you think: Relevance and reasoning in the selection task. *British Journal of Psychology, 87*, 223–240.

Evans, J. S. B. T. (1998). Matching bias in conditional reasoning: Do we understand it after 25 years? *Thinking and Reasoning, 4*, 45–82.

Evans, J. S. B. T. (2006). The heuristic-analytic theory of reasoning: Extension and evaluation. *Psychonomic Bulletin and Review, 13*, 378–395.

Evans, J. S. B. T. (2007). On the resolution of conflict in dual process theories of reasoning. *Thinking and Reasoning, 13*, 378–395.

Evans, J. S. B. T. and Ball, L. J. (2010). Do people reason on the Wason selection task? A new look at the data of Ball et al. (2003). *Quarterly Journal of Experimental Psychology, 63*, 434–441.

Evans, J. S. B. T., Ball, L. J. and Brooks, P. G. (1987). Attentional bias and decision order in a reasoning task. *British Journal of Psychology, 78*, 385–394.

Evans, J. S. B. T., Barston, J. L. and Pollard, P. (1983). On the conflict between logic and belief in syllogistic reasoning. *Memory and Cognition, 11*, 295–306.

Evans, J. S. B. T. and Lynch, J. S. (1973). Matching bias in the selection task. *British Journal of Psychology, 64*, 391–397.

Evans, J. S. B. T. and Stanovich, K. E. (2013). Dual-process theories of higher cognition: Advancing the debate. *Perspectives on Psychological Science, 8*, 223–241.

Evans, J. S. B. T. and Wason, P. W. (1976). Rationalization in a reasoning task. *British Journal of Psychology, 67*, 479–486.

Ferguson, H. J. and Sanford, A. J. (2008). Anomalies in real and counterfactual worlds: An eye-movement investigation. *Journal of Memory and Language, 58*, 609–626.

Goel, V. and Dolan, R. J. (2003). Explaining modulation of reasoning by belief. *Cognition, 87*, B11–B22.

Goldberg, H. J. and Wichansky, A. M. (2003). Eye tracking in usability evaluation: A practitioner's guide. In J. Hyönä, R. Radach and H. Deubel (Eds.), *The Mind's Eye: Cognitive and Applied Aspects of Eye Movement Research* (pp. 493–516). Amsterdam, The Netherlands: Elsevier.

Gladwell, M. (2005). *Blink.* London, UK: Penguin.

Grant, E. R. and Spivey, M. J. (2003). Eye movements and problem solving: Guiding attention guides thought. *Psychological Science*, *14*, 462–466.

Haigh, M., Stewart, A. J. and Connell, L. (2013). Reasoning as we read: Establishing the probability of causal conditionals. *Memory and Cognition*, *41*, 152–158.

He, P. and Kowler, E. (1992). The role of saccades in the perception of texture patterns. *Vision Research*, *32*, 2151–2163.

Hoffman, J. E. and Subramaniam, B. (1995). The role of visual attention in saccadic eye movements. *Perception and Psychophysics*, *57*, 787–795.

Hornikx, J. and Hahn, U. (2012). Reasoning and argumentation: Towards an integrated psychology of argumentation. *Thinking and Reasoning*, *18*, 225–243.

Jacob, R. J. K. and Karn, K. S. (2003). Eye tracking in Human-Computer Interaction and usability research: Ready to deliver the promises, In J. Hyönä, R. Radach and H. Deubel (Eds.), *The Mind's Eye: Cognitive and Applied Aspects of Eye Movement Research* (pp. 573–605). Amsterdam, The Netherlands: Elsevier.

Jones, G. (2003). Testing two cognitive theories of insight. *Journal of Experimental Psychology: Learning, Memory and Cognition*, *29*, 1017–1027.

Just, M. A. and Carpenter, P. A. (1976). Eye fixations and cognitive processes. *Cognitive Psychology*, *8*, 441–480.

Knoblich, G., Ohlsson, S., Haider, H. and Rhenius, D. (1999). Constraint relaxation and chunk decomposition in insight problem solving. *Journal of Experimental Psychology: Learning, Memory and Cognition*, *25*, 1534–1555.

Knoblich, G., Ohlsson, S. and Raney, G. E. (2001). An eye movement study of insight problem solving. *Memory and Cognition*, *29* (7), 1000–1009.

Kowler, E., Anderson, E., Dosher, B. and Blaser, E. (1995). The role of attention in the programming of saccades. *Vision Research*, *35*, 1897–1916.

Liversedge, S. P., Paterson, K. B. and Pickering, M. (1998). Eye movements and measures of reading time. In G. Underwood (Ed.), *Eye Guidance in Reading and Scene Perception*. Oxford, UK: Elsevier Science.

Litchfield, D. and Ball, L. J. (2011). Using another's gaze as an explicit aid to insight problem solving. *Quarterly Journal of Experimental Psychology*, *64*, 649–656.

Lucas, E. J. and Ball, L. J. (2005). Think-aloud protocols and the selection task: Evidence for relevance effects and rationalization processes. *Thinking and Reasoning*, *11*, 35–66.

Luo, J., Liu, X., Stupple, E. J., Zhang, E., Xiao, X., Jia, L., Yang, Q., Li, H. and Zhang, Q. (in press). Cognitive control in belief-laden reasoning during conclusion processing: An ERP study. *International Journal of Psychology*.

Morsanyi, K. and Handley, S. J. (2012). Logic feels so good –I like it! Evidence for intuitive detection of logicality in syllogistic reasoning. *Journal of Experimental Psychology: Learning, Memory and Cognition*, *38*, 596–616.

Newstead, S. E., Handley, S. J., Harley, C., Wright, H. and Farelly, D. (2004). Individual differences in deductive reasoning. *Quarterly Journal of Experimental Psychology*, *57A*, 33–60.

Oakhill, J. and Johnson-Laird, P. N. (1985). The effect of belief on the spontaneous production of syllogistic conclusions. *Quarterly Journal of Experimental Psychology*, *37A*, 553–570.

Oakhill, J., Johnson-Laird, P. N. and Garnham, A. (1989). Believability and syllogistic reasoning. *Cognition*, *31*, 117–140.

Ormerod, T. C. and Ball, L. J. (2007). Qualitative methods in cognitive psychology. In C. Willig and W. Stainton-Rogers (Eds.), *Handbook of Qualitative Research in Psychology* (pp. 553–574). London, UK: Sage Publications Ltd.

Pitchford, M. (2013). *Advancing an Understanding of Belief Bias through an Analysis of Individual Differences*. Unpublished PhD Thesis, Lancaster University, UK.

Pohl, R. (Ed.) (2004). *Cognitive Illusions: A Handbook on Fallacies and Biases in Thinking, Judgement and Memory*. Hove, UK: Psychology Press.

Poole, A. and Ball, L. J. (2006). Eye tracking in HCI and usability research. In C. Ghaoui (Ed.), *Encyclopedia of Human-Computer Interaction* (pp. 211–219). Hershey, PA: Idea Group, Inc.

Prowse Turner, J. A. and Thompson, V. A. (2009). The role of training, alternative models and logical necessity in determining confidence in syllogistic reasoning. *Thinking and Reasoning*, *15*, 69–100.

Quayle, J. D. and Ball, L. J. (2000). Working memory, metacognitive uncertainty and belief bias in syllogistic reasoning. *Quarterly Journal of Experimental Psychology*, *53A*, 1202–1223.

Rayner, K. (1998). Eye movements in reading and information processing: 20 years of research. *Psychological Bulletin*, *124*, 372–422.

Roberts, M. J. (1998). Inspection times and the selection task: Are they relevant? *Quarterly Journal of Experimental Psychology*, *51A*, 781–810.

Roberts, M. J. and Newton, E. J. (2011). Rapid-response versus free-time selection tasks using different logical connectives. *Journal of Cognitive Psychology*, *23*, 858–872.

Sá, W. C., West, R. F. and Stanovich, K. E. (1999). The domain specificity and generality of belief bias: Searching for a generalizable critical thinking skill. *Journal of Educational Psychology*, 91, 497–510.

Schaeken, W., De Voogt, G., Vandierendonck, A. and d'Ydewalle, G. (1999). *Deductive Reasoning and Strategies*. Mahwah, NJ: Lawrence Erlbaum Associates, Inc.

Sclingensiepen, K. H., Campbell, F. W., Legge, G. E. and Walker, T. D. (1986). The importance of eye movements in the analysis of simple patterns. *Vision Research*, *26*, 1111–1117.

Sloman, S. A. (2002). Two systems of reasoning. In T. Gilovich, D. Griffin and D. Kahneman (Eds.), *Heuristics and Biases: The Psychology of Intuitive Judgment* (pp. 379–398). Cambridge, UK: Cambridge University Press.

Stanovich, K. E. (2009). Distinguishing the reflective, algorithmic, and autonomous minds: Is it time for a tri-process theory? In J. S. B. T. Evans and K. Frankish (Eds.), *In Two Minds: Dual Processes and Beyond* (pp. 55–88). Oxford, UK: Oxford University Press.

Stanovich, K. E. and West, R. F. (1997). Reasoning independently of prior belief and individual differences in actively open minded thinking. *Journal of Educational Psychology*, 89, 342–357.

Stanovich, K. E. and West, R. F. (1998). Cognitive ability and variation in selection task performance. *Thinking and Reasoning*, *4*, 193–230.

Stanovich, K. E. and West, R. F. (2000). Individual differences in reasoning: Implications for the rationality debate. *Behavioral and Brain Sciences*, *23*, 645–726.

Stanovich, K. E., West, R. F. and Toplak, M. (2011). Individual differences as essential components of heuristics and biases research. In K. I. Manktelow, D. E. Over and S. Elqayam (Eds.), *The Science of Reason: A Festschrift for Jonathan St. B. T Evans* (pp. 355–396). Hove, UK: Psychology Press.

Stewart, A. J., Haigh, M. and Ferguson, H. J. (2013). Sensitivity to speaker control in the online comprehension of conditional tips and promises: an eye-tracking study. *Journal of Experimental Psychology: Learning, Memory and Cognition*, *39*, 1022–1036.

Stupple, E. J. N. and Ball, L. J. (2008). Belief-logic conflict resolution in syllogistic reasoning: Inspection-time evidence for a parallel-process model. *Thinking and Reasoning*, *14*, 168–181.

Stupple, E.J. N., Ball, L. J., Evans, J. St. B. T. and Kamal-Smith, E. N. (2011). When logic and belief collide: Individual differences in reasoning times support a selective processing model. *Journal of Cognitive Psychology*, *23*, 931–941.

Thompson, V. A. and Evans, J. S. B. T. (2012). Belief bias in informal reasoning. *Thinking and Reasoning*, *18*, 278–310.

Thompson, V. A., Morley, N. J. and Newstead, S. E. (2011). Methodological and theoretical issues in belief-bias: Implications for dual process theories. In K. I. Manktelow, D. E. Over and S. Elqayam (Eds.), *The Science of Reason: A Festschrift for Jonathan St. B. T Evans* (pp. 309–338). Hove, UK: Psychology Press.

Thompson, V. A., Striemer, C. L., Reikoff, R., Gunter, R. W. and Campbell, J. D. (2003). Syllogistic reasoning time: Disconfirmation disconfirmed. *Psychonomic Bulletin and Review*, *10*, 184–189.

Wade, N. J. and Tatler, B. W. (2011). Origins and applications of eye movement research. In S. P. Liversedge, I. D. Gilchrist and S. Everling (Eds.), *Oxford Handbook of Eye Movements* (pp. 17–43). Oxford, UK: Oxford University Press.

Wason, P.C. (1966). Reasoning. In B. M. Foss (Ed.), *New Horizons in Psychology* (Vol. I). Harmondsworth, UK: Penguin.

Wason, P.C. and Johnson-Laird, P. N. (1972). *Psychology of Reasoning: Structure and Content*. London, UK: Batsford.

6 Self-perception and reasoning

How perceiving yourself as rational makes you less biased

Maria Augustinova

Summary

Research on reasoning and decision-making has amply documented that human thinking is usually biased because people rely on their intuition instead of using more analytical thinking. In this chapter I argue that this tendency can be significantly attenuated by transient changes in people's self-perception called working self-concept (Markus and Nurius, 1986; Markus and Ruvolo, 1989). To this end, I first detail this notion and then provide review of existing literature suggesting its general influence on information processing. I conclude this chapter with considering implications of this work for research on base rate sensitivity and thinking and reasoning in general.

Introduction

Social psychological research has amply documented the fact that people tend to view themselves in terms of characteristics that are positive or believed to lead to success (see e.g., Alicke and Govorun, 2005; Dunning, 1999; Markus and Kunda, 1986; Pyszczynski and Greenberg, 1987; Taylor and Brown, 1988 for reviews).

For instance, Kunda and her colleagues induced university students to believe that either extraversion or introversion is related to academic and professional success. In the subsequent self-perception task, the students who were led to believe that extraversion is conducive to success then rated themselves as more extraverted and less introverted than the participants induced to believe the opposite (Kunda, 1987; Kunda and Sanitioso, 1989; Sanitioso, Kunda and Fong, 1990).

To some, such changes may simply reflect blatant self-presentation also known as impression management (see e.g., Goffmann, 2002; Schlenker, 1980). According to such views, these students simply present themselves in a favorable light without necessarily believing to possess the aforementioned success-conducive attributes.

However, research on self and identity suggests that a powerful psychological device called *working self-concept* (Markus and Ruvolo, 1989; Markus and Nurius, 1986) enables people to genuinely believe in the possession of attributes leading to success. The working self-concept is achieved by the temporary presence on people's minds of self-knowledge that confirms the desired self-perception (Brunot and Sanitioso, 2004; Markus and Kunda, 1986; Sanitioso and Niedenthal, 2006; see also e.g., Sanitioso, Conway and Brunot, 2006 for a review). This means that past personal experiences or behaviors consistent with introversion (e.g., difficulty in making new friends when first arriving on campus, leaving a party full of unknown people etc.) became increasingly active in the students who were led to believe that introversion is conducive to success. On the basis of this authentic self-knowledge, people are then able to adjust their momentary self-conception toward success-conducive attributes.

Moreover, the working self-concept is thought to regulate people's behavior (see e.g., Markus and Kunda, 1986; Markus and Wurf, 1987; Sanitioso, 1998). This line of research suggests that not only do people flexibly adjust their self-perception to different situational or social demands but they also tend to behave in agreement with their newly achieved working self-concept. Imagine for instance your single, middle-aged friend who is eager to meet somebody browsing on a dating website. If he/she comes across a potential dating partner looking for an outgoing and intelligent soul mate interested in literature, it is likely that, when i-chatting with this person, he/she will tend to talk about books in a lively and smart way. Again, the content and the form of the chat will be modeled by the relevant self-knowledge present on your friend's mind corresponding to sometimes very distant memories such as being a member of a high school book club.

In this chapter I will extend this robust social psychological finding on reasoning. More specifically, I will argue that classic reasoning biases can be attenuated as easily as making people believe that a reliance on reason and facts in their everyday judgments and decisions is conducive to success. Indeed, as explained above, such belief leads people to adjust their working self-concept accordingly and consequently adopt more analytical thinking. As such, they will be less biased in their probabilistic reasoning. Before presenting empirical research supporting such an idea, I will first detail the notion of the working self-concept and its cognitive underpinnings, and examine its influence on information processing. I will conclude this chapter by considering some potential explanations of how the working self-concept influences people's reasoning and by examining some broader implications of this work.

Working self-concept and its influence on information processing

As mentioned previously, *working self-concept* (Markus and Ruvolo, 1989; Markus and Nurius, 1986; but see also Conway and Pleydell-Pearce, 2000 for a slightly different use of this term) enables people to perceive themselves in terms of characteristics that allow them to come across as an ideal dating partner, a desirable job applicant, a successful parent . . . in short as *the right person in the right place*. In the following section I will provide more details about how such desired self-perceptions are achieved and in what way they influence people's subsequent thinking and behavior.

Construction and maintenance of the working self-concept

The process of self-construal (i.e., construction and maintenance of the working self-concept, Peters and Gawronski, 2011) is an epistemic process grounded in *autobiographical memory* (see Conway and Pleydell-Pearce, 2000; Conway, Singer and Tagini, 2004). Remember that, throughout our lives, we accumulate abundant knowledge about ourselves called *self-concept* (see Markus, 1977). Yet many instances of our self-knowledge stored in this part of our memory are clearly contradictory. For example, many people will have had the experience of being charming and funny at friends' parties and grumpy and dry at family gatherings. Thus, despite the general stability of the knowledge people have about themselves (e.g., whether they are extraverted or introverted for instance), the elements of our self-concept that are accessible at any given time (i.e., working self-concept biased toward extraversion or introversion) clearly depend on the self-relevant objectives that are currently being processed (Conway and Pleydell-Pearce, 2000; Markus and Kunda, 1986; Markus and Nurius, 1986; Markus and Ruvolo, 1989).

In the work of Kunda and colleagues mentioned above, participants' self-relevant objective was to assert the validity of an idea about themselves as being either extraverted or introverted (i.e., as possessing success-conducive attributes). According to Peters and Gawronski (2011), this "hypothesis-driven" (also called *top-down*) self-construal process is generally biased towards positive testing of such an idea (see also Kunda, 1990). Consequently, when autobiographical memory is searched for relevant evidence, not only do instances of self-knowledge that confirm the desired self-perception become increasingly accessible (see above) but instances that disconfirm such self-perception become inhibited (Brunot and Sanitioso, 2004; Markus and Kunda, 1986; Sanitioso and Niedenthal, 2006; see also Sanitioso at al., 2006 for a review). In sum, our working self-concept is achieved and maintained by genuine self-associations congruent with the desired attribute.

Recent research by Peters and Gawronski (2011, Experiment 2) demonstrates this very issue. These researchers first replicated the above-mentioned (i.e., explicit) changes in participants' self-concepts observed by Kunda and colleagues. Then they submitted their participants to an Implicit Association Test (Greenwald and Farnham, 2000) measuring the strength of associations between different concepts in people's memory. This procedure requires people to rapidly categorize two target concepts with an attribute (e.g. the concepts "male" and "female" with the attribute "competent"). Keep in mind that easier pairings (for which faster responses occur e.g., male–competent) are interpreted as more strongly associated in memory than more difficult pairings (for which slower responses occur e.g., female–competent).

This measure of participants' implicit working self-concept complimented the results of the explicit measure. Participants who were led to believe that extraversion is conducive to success consequently responded more rapidly when associating self with items related to extraversion (e.g. pairing me–extraverted) compared to introversion (e.g., pairing me–introverted); whereas those who were led to believe that introversion is conducive to success consequently responded more rapidly when associating self with items related to introversion compared to extraversion.

To sum up, the working self-concept is highly responsive to contextual demands combined with one's own personal needs. Because the ensuing changes in individuals' working self-concept are firmly grounded in the authentic self-knowledge stored in individuals' autobiographic memory, these changes occur without any feelings of inconsistency or inauthenticity (see e.g., Swann and Bosson, 2010; Swann, Bosson and Pelham, 2002).

Cognitive consequences of the working self-concept

An extensive amount of research has shown that once a working self-concept achieved, it subsequently influences processing of different kinds of self-related information (e.g., Brunot and Sanitioso, 2004; Sanitioso, 1998, 2008; Sanitioso et al., 1990; Sanitioso and Niedenthal, 2006; see also Sanitioso et al., 2006). For instance, after an initial experiment that exactly replicated the above-mentioned work of Kunda and her colleagues, Sanitioso and Wlodarski (2004) gave their participants false feedback about their extra- and introversion. In a surprise recall task, extraversion–success participants remembered extraversion feedback more accurately than their counterparts, and introversion–success participants remembered introversion feedback more accurately than their counterparts. In sum, such studies clearly indicate that the working self-concept influences the processing of self-relevant information.

However, research dedicated to the question of whether the working self-concept influences processing of information that is unrelated in content to the self is still in its infancy. Preliminary answers to this question come from contiguous research on self-definition originating from cross-cultural social psychology (see e.g., Markus and Kitayama, 1991). Broadly speaking, self-definition incorporates self–other relationships into the representation of the self. According to this line of research, people define themselves either in terms of relationships with other individuals or groups or as an autonomous entity. The former is called *interdependent*, the latter *independent self-definition*. Even though this culturally rooted self-definition is rather stable,[1] exactly like the working self-concept, it is also malleable[2] and varies as a function of a surrounding context and its specific demands (see e.g., Oyserman and Sorensen, 2009; Vogeley and Roepstorff, 2009 for review).

This line of research showed that momentary self-definition influences the way people process different kinds of self-unrelated information such ambiguous visual stimuli (Kühnen, Hannover and Schubert, 2001; Kühnen and Oyserman, 2002; Lin and Han, 2009; Lin, Lin and Han, 2008; Springer, Beyer, Derrfuss, Volz and Hannover, 2012; see also e.g., Oyserman and Lee, 2008 for review). For instance, in one of their studies, Kühnen and Oyserman (2002) first exposed psychology students to the concept of interdependence or interdependence through the procedure called *priming*. The students read a brief paragraph about a trip to a city, and were instructed to circle all the pronouns in the text. In the interdependence priming condition the pronouns represented the interdependent self (e.g., we, our, us), while in the independence priming condition, the pronouns represented the individual self (e.g., I, me, mine). Then they were presented with a series of compound letters (i.e., an upper case "H" consisting itself of lower case "F"s). For each compound letter, they were asked to recognize as quickly as possible the letter (half of the time upper case and half of the time lower) presented on the screen. Note that that quick recognition of the lower case F does not necessitate taking into account the relationship between different letters presented on the screen, in contrast to recognizing the upper case H. In line with such reasoning, psychology students primed with independence recognized the lower case letters faster than they recognized the upper case letters (made up of these lower caseletters), while the opposite was observed in psychology students primed with interdependence (see also Lin and Han, 2009; Lin et al., 2008).

More relatedly to the issue of reasoning, Kim, Grimm and Markman (2007) extended the influence of momentary perception of the self as independent vs. interdependent to the processing of *covariation information.* To understand what covariation information is, imagine that a consumer organization (CO) wishes to evaluate whether a particular facial serum, advertised as an overnight miracle, indeed rejuvenates women's complexion. To this end, the CO gives the serum to 20 of our 40 women and the remaining half receive a placebo product instead. 15 out of 20 women receiving the serum report their complexion to be rejuvenated in the morning, whereas only 5 out of 20 women not receiving the serum report the same result. Hence the probability for the serum to produce the advertised miracle is .50 (15/20 –5/20 = 10/20) meaning that it is a fairly effective and probably worth its (high) price. However, right before publishing the report the CO realizes that, by mistake, the same panel of women were simultaneously involved in the testing of another cosmetic product (e.g., a night cream) advertised as causing the same effect. Thus to make absolutely sure that the serum is effective, the CO should examine its effect both in the presence and in the absence of the cream (i.e., to control for the effect of the cream). However, when people identify a cause that seems to reliably produce an effect, they often fail to conditionalize their judgments on an alternative.

Now, consider the results of this additional check as shown in Table 6.1.

As you can see, all the women who also used the cream (left column) report a rejuvenated face in the morning (15/20 + 5/20 = 20/20) independently of whether they have used the serum. However, among the women who hadn't used the cream (right column), none reports such result (0/5 + 0/15 = 0/20). This means

Table 6.1 Example covariation information.

		Cream	
		Used	*Not used*
Serum	*Used*	15*/15	0/5
	Not used	5/5	0/15

* Note: The numerator represents the number of times that women report rejuvenated complexion.

that contrary to the first conclusion, the serum itself has absolutely no effect on women's glow. It just seems to have an effect because of the way the application of the two products *covaries*. Indeed, there were more women who had used or hadn't used both facial products simultaneously than those who have used or not used just one product. Because attending to this contextual information influences people's successful reasoning in this task (by broadly making them more inclined to check whether the serum is effective in both the presence and absence of the cream), Kim et al. (2007) expected individuals primed with interdependence to do better on this task than those primed with independence. Recall that individuals primed with interdependence are more likely to take into account the existing relations between different pieces of available information than those primed with independence.

To test this hypothesis, the individuals participating in the study were first exposed to the previously depicted priming task used by Kühnen and Oyserman (2002). Then they were presented with several problems similar to the aforementioned example. Participants' ratings of the effectiveness of both causes (e.g., serum and cream) on the effect (e.g., rejuvenated skin) somewhat confirmed their general hypothesis: relative to individuals primed with an independence, those primed with interdependence showed a greater propensity to conditionalize their judgments on an alternative cause. However, since both groups showed biases in their causal judgments (although in different directions), the authors were reluctant to conclude that individuals viewing themselves as interdependent were more accurate in their causal reasoning than are those viewing themselves as independent. Thus, whether the momentary perception of the self (i.e., a particular self-definition or a working self-concept) can actually promote more accurate reasoning (i.e., reasoning that is closer to unambiguous normative standards) still remains an open issue. Consequently, my colleagues and I (Augustinova, Collange, Sanitioso and Musca, 2011) attempted to address this issue by using a different reasoning paradigm which is less prone to the outlined ambiguities.

Self-perception in terms of rationality and probabilistic reasoning

Our work is rooted in the theoretical perspective called *dual-process framework*, which postulates the existence of two distinct systems (often called System 1 and 2) that people may use to solve a problem (e.g., Barbey and Sloman, 2007; Epstein, 1990, 1994; Evans and Over, 1996; Kahneman and Frederick, 2002, 2005; Sloman, 1996; Stanovich and West, 2000). According to this perspective, System 1 tends to solve a problem heuristically by relying on prior knowledge and beliefs. It is thought to be rapid, automatic and effortless. System 2 allows reasoning according to logical standards. It is thought to be slow, controlled and requiring cognitive effort.

The extent to which people preferentially rely on one of these two systems in their everyday reasoning and decision-making is called a *thinking style*. The Rational-Experiential Inventory (Epstein, Pacini, Denes-Raj and Heier, 1996) allows for assessing whether individuals' thinking style is *experiential* (i.e., they preferentially use System 1) or *rational* (i.e., they preferentially use System 2). Broadly speaking, to reason and solve problems, some people prefer to expend a considerable cognitive effort (e.g., in the aforementioned inventory for instance, they strongly agree with propositions like "I tend to set goals that can be accomplished only by expending considerable mental effort." [Epstein et al., 1996, p. 394]). Other people prefer to trust their hunches and intuition without overthinking things (e.g., not only do they strongly disagree with the latter proposition but also tend to strongly agree with propositions like "When it comes to trusting people, I can usually rely on my gut feelings." [Epstein et al., 1996, p. 394]).

This line of research showed that in the classic problems used by researchers studying reasoning and decision-making, responses considered as normatively correct are positively predicted by people's rational cognitive style and negatively predicted by their experiential cognitive style (Klaczynski, Gordon and Fauth, 1997; Shiloh, Salton and Sharabi, 2002; Witteman, van den Bercken, Claes and Godoy, 2009; see also Epstein, 2003; Pacini and Epstein, 1999b; Pacini, Muir and Epstein, 1998). Consequently, we wanted to examine whether the extent to which people are biased in their reasoning can also be influenced by the way they momentarily perceive themselves in those rational vs. experiential terms (i.e., their working self-concept reflects those qualities).

Description of the basic research paradigm

More specifically, in four studies, we wanted to assess the extent to which manipulating the desirability of so-called rational (vs. intuitive) cognitive style leads not only to changes in temporary self-perception in those terms (as research presented in the previous section has shown) but also impacts the way people solve a classic decision-making problem called the *Lawyer-Engineer Problem* (Kahneman and Tversky, 1973).

This problem (hereafter referred to as the L-E problem) is indeed a key element of our paradigm since it easily and rather unambiguously captures the gap that exists between people's actual reasoning and normative standards. Indeed, the L-E problem was devised to illustrate the fact that in their probabilistic reasoning about particular situations or people, many individuals experience difficulties in using information about prior probabilities called *base rate information.* Consider one of the original formulations the L-E problem:

> Several psychologists interviewed a group of people. The group was made up of 30 per cent (*vs.*70) lawyers and 70 per cent (*vs.*30) engineers. The psychologists prepared a brief summary of their impression of each interviewee. The following description was drawn randomly from the set of descriptions:
>
> Dan is 45 years old. He is married and has four children. He is generally conservative, cautious and ambitious. He shows no interest in political and social issues and spends most of his free time on his many hobbies, which include home carpentry, sailing and mathematical puzzles.

When asked to estimate the chances out of 100 that Dan is an engineer, many people seem to give little weight to the normatively relevant information about the relative frequencies of lawyers and engineers in the sample (i.e., base rates). Bluntly put, they seem to disregard the size of each group in the sample. Instead they approach this task intuitively by evaluating the extent to which the information about Dan is representative of categories they are considering (i.e., lawyers vs. engineers). As a result, they estimate the probability that a man "having no interest in political issues and spending most of his free time on his hobbies, including mathematical puzzles" is an engineer as consistently high.

This intuitive response based on representativeness certainly yields reasonable judgments in control (i.e., congruent) problems in which base rates (e.g., 70 per cent) and the description of Dan cue the same response. But it clearly leads to incorrect judgments in the crucial incongruent problems (i.e., problems in which the individual description conflicts with the low base rates). Indeed, if only 30 per cent of the sample are engineers, it will be more likely that a randomly drawn description will the one of a lawyer.

Another important feature of this task is that people's probability estimates provide scientists with some information about *how* people reason. Indeed, within the dual-process framework (see above), the representative response is assumed to result from the use of System 1 that for the ease of presentation I will call an *intuitive system* (but see e.g., Inbar, Cone and Gilovich, 2010 for the distinction between rational and intuitive system). The base rate response on the other hand is assumed to be the product of System 2 or a *rational* system. Since the adequate solution of incongruent problems requires the use of base rates, it is essential for the rational system to override the tempting intuitive response based on representativeness cued by the intuitive system. Our work was designed to test the general hypothesis that this is the most likely to happen in individuals with *rational* working self-concept.

To this end, participants in our studies were asked to participate in a series of independent studies in educational psychology. In reality, these studies corresponded to the three distinct sections of the experimental protocol: induction of desirability of rational vs. intuitive thinking styles; assessment of people's working self-concept; and L-E problem solving. The first two parts of the protocol were modeled after the previously mentioned work of Kunda and colleagues such that the participants were led to believe that individuals with a particular cognitive style experience more or less success. In Experiment 1 for instance, our participants (all first-year psychology students) were presented with a fictitious scientific study that reads as follows:

> In an extensive longitudinal study, an interdisciplinary research group [. . .] wished to examine the predictors of academic and professional success among psychology students. [. . .] Using a large array of tests and scales, researchers performed a comprehensive assessment of each participating individual, while also tracking their academic and professional achievements throughout the ten years that followed his/her enrollment in the psychology program.

> The most novel findings of this study relate to individuals' general disposition (also called cognitive style) towards either rationality or intuition. More specifically, it showed that psychology students with a rational (vs. intuitive) cognitive style (i.e., one characterized by a high reliance on reason and facts [vs. instincts and feelings] in their everyday judgments and decisions) achieve more (vs. less) academic and professional success. Indeed, they tend to have higher (vs. lower) grades and thus are more (vs. less) likely to be accepted into graduate programs than students characterized by a highly intuitive (vs. rational) style. A rational (vs. intuitive) cognitive style also constitutes an advantage (vs. disadvantage) in their early professional careers: they are more (vs. less) highly regarded by their superiors and tend to have more (vs. less) stable and rewarding professional careers.
>
> These findings are unrelated to the participants' other characteristics (such as IQ for instance).

Given that people usually trust their own observations they explain to themselves (see, e.g., Anderson, Lepper and Ross, 1980; Anderson and Sechler, 1986), the participants in our study were asked to use their own experience and knowledge to explain why the findings of the scientific study might be true.

The subsequent task was designed to assess the extent to which participants changed their working self-concepts toward dimensions previously described as conductive to success. In other words, we wanted to evaluate the extent to which participants achieved a rational vs. intuitive working self-concept. This part was presented as an unrelated study to participants. For instance, Experiment 2, using business students enrolled in Organizational Behavior class as participants, was presented as a class activity involving personality assessment in organizations. It required them to assess their personality on 25 different traits (listed in alphabetical order) including three that were rationality related (i.e., rational, logical, reflective) and three that were intuition related (i.e., intuitive, spontaneous, instinctive) traits. Participants responded using five-point Likert-type scales (0 = not at all me; 4 = very much me).

Finally, after having agreed to participate in another unrelated study, participants were asked to solve the L-E problem type of problems. For instance, in Experiment 4 they were asked to solve eight problems, similar to those used by De Neys and colleagues (see De Neys and Glumicic, 2008 for more details), that were presented randomly on a computer screen. For instance, before the participants were asked to estimate the chances out of 100 that a person described is a doctor, they learned that:

> A group of 100 people including 69 nurses and 31 doctors was tested. The following description was randomly drawn from the descriptions of each participant:
>
> Pierre is 52 years old. He is elegant and well spoken. He likes modern art and fancies its auctions. His tastefully furbished house is situated in a posh suburb.

As explained earlier, the individual description provided in this problem is stereotypically associated with a category with the low base rates. Said differently, the fact that Pierre sounds like a doctor conflicts with the low proportions of doctors in the tested group. Our participants were given four of these congruent problems and four incongruent problems. Remember that the individual description provided in these latter problems is stereotypically associated with a category with the high base rates.

Main findings

The analysis of participants' ratings on rationality- and intuition-related traits showed that the participants who were led to believe that rationality is conducive to academic success (or intuition conducive to academic failure) perceived themselves as more rational and less intuitive than the participants induced to believe the opposite. In short, their desire to view themselves in terms of attributes leading to personal success caused them to adjust their temporary self-perceptions of their own rational or intuitive natures.

More importantly, when examining the difference between the mean score on traits related to rationality and those related to intuition – a measure of working self-concept – this measure accurately predicted peoples' performance in the L-E task that followed. More precisely, individuals with rational working self-concepts relied more on base rates in their reasoning (i.e., their probability estimates were closer to the stated base-rates), compared to those with intuitive working self-concepts. Importantly, the reliance on the rational system in critical incongruent problems (as evidenced by both the use of base rates and the longer times to make their decisions) was specifically due to a stronger rational working self-concept (as confirmed by a statistical technique called *meditational analysis*). In other words, the more people's temporary self-perceptions shifted towards rationality, the greater was their subsequent preference for using a rational system (over an intuitive system) during reasoning.

In sum, results from these studies suggest a theoretically plausible causal chain, for example, the desire to possess success-conducive (or failure-avoidant) attributes leads people to adjust their working self-concept in terms of rationality. This newly created self-view subsequently influences people's tendency to adopt a rational reasoning system (i.e., a system that involves more effortful and analytical processing which results in greater reliance on base rates).

Broader implications for thinking and reasoning research

The most obvious and immediate question raised by the studies presented in this chapter is how exactly the working self-concept makes people to adopt a rational reasoning system? As briefly discussed in our paper (Augustinova et al., 2011), my colleagues and I believe that individuals with the rational working self-concept rely on base rates because they were particularly efficient in *inhibiting* the intuitive appeal of representativeness.

Such interpretation is rooted in a particular idea about how the two systems of reasoning interact. Indeed, if there is a consensus among dual-process theorists about the main features of each system (see above), there is clearly a lack of agreement about their interplay (see e.g., Evans, 2003; Osman, 2004). Some researchers (Evans, 1984, 2003; Kahneman, 2002 cited by De Neys, Vartanian and Goel, 2008) consider that people use an intuitive system as a default option and that the role of a rational system is to monitor its output. However, these researchers typically also consider that this monitoring is not at all efficient. Thus, people's widespread reliance on representativeness is interpreted as a failure of the rational system to detect the conflict between the intuitive response and the one favored by probability. This means that in the previously described problem depicting Pierre, people do not even notice that the response cued by the fact that Pierre looks very much like a doctor conflicts with the low proportions of doctors in the tested group. Other dual-process theorists (Denes-Raj and Epstein, 1994; De Neys, 2006a, 2006b; Epstein, 1990, 1994; Pacini and Epstein, 1999; Sloman, 1996) consider that people are quite effective in detecting. In their view, the pervasiveness of intuitive thinking results from a failure to inhibit (rather than to detect or monitor) intuitive responses resulting from representativeness (see De Neys et al., 2008 for detailed discussion). To summarize, in the first view people do not know that they are biased, whereas in the second view, they know that they are, but very often cannot help it.

De Neys and colleagues (2008, see also e.g., De Neys and Goel, 2011) nicely demonstrated the viability of this second view in a study where they monitored the brain activity of participants solving the L-E type of problems. They observed that brain regions known to mediate conflict-detection (i.e., an area called the *anterior cingulate cortex*) specifically responded to incongruent (as compared to congruent) base-rate problems regardless of whether participants' responses in these incongruent problems resulted from the use of base rates or representativeness. However, another brain area known to mediate inhibitory processing (i.e., the *right lateral prefrontal cortex*) was activated only when participants avoided responses resulting from representativeness on such incongruent problems.

Note that this latter finding (see also e.g., Aron, Robbins and Poldrack, 2004; Forstmann, Jahfari, Scholte, Wolfensteller, van den Wildenberg and Ridderinkhof, 2008) is crucial for our interpretation. It suggests that the quite spectacular reliance on base rates exhibited by our participants when arbitrary induced with rational working self-concept is due to their increased capacity to inhibit tempting intuitive responses. The fact that the increased reliance on base rates was specifically linked to the rational working self-concept in incongruent problems that call for inhibition of intuitive beliefs is indeed consistent with such a possibility. Moreover, independently of their working self-concept, all participants exhibited longer decision times for incongruent compared to congruent problems. Taken together these results suggest that all participants were quite successful in detecting the conflict between the intuitive response and the one favored by probability but only those with rational working self-concept were also successful in inhibiting the tempting intuitive response. Thus these results also contribute to the aforementioned debate among the interplay between the two systems of reasoning.

Of course other interpretations of our findings are possible. Cassotti and Moutier (2010) suggest, for instance, that people are more or less efficient emotion-based learners and that their capacity for rational reasoning is linked to an ability to perceive emotional warning signals that gradually lead them to avoid disadvantageous decisions. Given that our participants are not only motivated to achieve but also to maintain their success-conducive (or failure-avoidant) self-concept, it is plausible that the mismatch between their rational working self-concept and tempting intuitive belief amplifies such emotional warning signals and/or facilitates their perception. It is also plausible that in order to maintain their current self-concept, people selectively attend (or give more weight) to information that is consistent with their self-perception and that they attend less to information that is inconsistent with it (see e.g., Sanitioso and Wlodarski, 2004). Within such a perspective, it is plausible that for people with rational working self-concept, intuitive responses are simply much less tempting because they are irrelevant or even threatening to their endeavor to sustain their current working self-concept. It should be noted that these explanations do not contradict but rather complement the inhibition account. Indeed, it may be easier to inhibit information that is perceived as less tempting or relevant.

As a side note, I would like to mention that the current research on cognitive consequences of momentary self-definition as independent vs. interdependent of other people that I previously discussed, also seems to indicate the viability of the inhibition-based explanatory account. As I explained, these self-definitions determine the way people process different kinds of self-unrelated information such as ambiguous visual stimuli or covariation information. Interestingly, Springer and colleagues (2012) have recently argued that this influence is at least in part due to the fact that individuals' momentary self-definitions influence the extent to which they successfully inhibit information that is irrelevant for the task they are doing. Note that alternative explanations in the self-definition field (e.g., Han and Northoff, 2008; Hannover and Kühnen, 2009; Hannover, Pöhlmann, Springer and Röder, 2005; Oyserman and Sorensen, 2009) have been criticized (e.g., Kim et al., 2007). Hence, I believe that further development and refinement of the inhibitory account holds great promise for both the reasoning field and the work on the cognitive consequences of self-definitions.

Conclusion

To sum up, studies presented in this chapter are clearly consistent with the general idea that a classic reasoning bias such as *base rate neglect* can be attenuated as easily as making people believe that a reliance on reason and facts in their everyday judgments and decisions is conducive to success. Indeed, people's desire to view themselves in terms of attributes leading to personal success (or avoiding personal failure), through the working self-concept that it entails, influences their general information processing. Thus perceiving oneself in terms of attributes related to rationality seems to make people less biased in their reasoning.

Such a conclusion diverges from past research suggesting that it is difficult to improve people's reasoning. Such research showed indeed that tutoring people in logic does not change or changes only modestly the way people reason (see e.g., Kahneman, Slovic and Tversky, 1982; Kahneman and Tversky, 1996; Moutier and Houdé, 2003; Osman, 2007, see also e.g., Reyna and Farley, 2006; Steinberg, 2004, 2007). As pointed by De Neys et al. (2008), this lack of success might be due to the fact that these programs depart from the inccorect assumption that people lack statistical knowledge.

The reason why a "soft" or "indirect" procedure such as inducing people with a rational working self-concept outperforms these different "hard" or "direct" tutoring programs might be the simple fact that its primary goal is not to improve people's knowledge. Indeed, I believe that by incidentally improving people's inhibitory capacities (see also e.g., Cassotti and Moutier, 2010; Houdé, 2007) it simply allows people to take the full advantage of their already existing "rational sides".

Notes

1 Cross-cultural social psychology holds that individuals in collectivist cultures (e.g., African countries) tend to view theirselves as interdependent whereas those in individualistic cultures (e.g., Western European countries) as independent (see e.g., Cross, Bacon and Morris, 2000; Oyserman, Coon and Kemmelmeier, 2002 for reviews).

2 Obvious conceptual communalities between transitory self-definition (or construal) and working self-concept are still largely ignored (see Peters and Gawronski, 2011 as an exception).

References

Alicke, M. D. and Govorun, O. (2005). The better-than-average effect. In M. D. Alicke, D. A. Dunning and J. I. Krueger (Eds.), *The self in social judgment* (pp. 85–106). Philadelphia, PA: Psychology Press.

Anderson, C. A. and Sechler, E. S. (1986). Effects of explanation and counterexplanation on the development and use of statistical theories. *Journal of Personality and Social Psychology*, *50*, 24–34.

Anderson, C. A., Lepper, M. R. and Ross, L. (1980). Perseverance of social theories: The role of explanation in the persistence of discredited information. *Journal of Personality and Social Psychology*, *39*, 1037–1047.

Aron, A.R., Robbins, T.W. and Poldrack, R.A. (2004). Inhibition and the right inferior frontal cortex. *Trends in Cognitive Sciences*, *8*, 170–177.

Augustinova, M., Collange, J., Sanitioso, R. B and Musca, S.C. (2011). Power of the desired self: Influence of induced perceptions of the self on reasoning. *Cognition*, *121*, 299–312.

Barbey, A. K. and Sloman, S. A. (2007). Base-rate respect: From ecological rationality to dual processes. *Behavioral and Brain Sciences*, *30*, 241–254.

Brunot, S. and Sanitioso, R. (2004). Motivational influence on the quality of memories: Recall of general autobiographical memories related to desired attributes. *European Journal of Social Psychology*, *34*, 627–635.

Cassotti, M. and Moutier, S. (2010). How to explain receptivity to conjunction-fallacy inhibition training: Evidence from the Iowa Gambling Task. *Brain and Cognition, 72,* 378–384.

Conway, M. A. and Pleydell-Pearce, C. W. (2000). The construction of autobiographical memories in the self-memory system. *Psychological Review, 107,* 261–288.

Conway, M. A., Singer, J. A. and Tagini, A. (2004). The self and autobiographical memory: Correspondence and coherence. *Social Cognition, 22,* 491–529.

Cross, S. E., Bacon, P. and Morris, M. (2000). The relational-interdependent self-construal and relationships. *Journal of Personality and Social Psychology, 78,* 791–808.

Denes-Raj, V. and Epstein, S. (1994). Conflict between intuitive and rational processing: When people behave against their better judgment. *Journal of Personality and Social Psychology, 66,* 819–829.

De Neys, W. (2006a). Dual processing in reasoning: Two systems but one reasoner. *Psychological Science, 17,* 428–433.

De Neys, W. (2006b). Automatic-heuristic and executive-analytic processing in reasoning: Chronometric and dual task considerations. *Quarterly Journal of Experimental Psychology, 59,* 1070–1100.

De Neys, W. (2009). Beyond response output: More logical than we think. *Behavioral and Brain Sciences, 32,* 87–88.

De Neys, W. and Franssens, S. (2009). Belief inhibition during thinking: Not always winning but at least taking part. *Cognition, 113,* 45–61.

De Neys, W. and Glumicic, T. (2008). Conflict monitoring in dual process theories of thinking. *Cognition, 106* (3), 1248–1299.

De Neys, W. and Goel, V. (2011). Heuristics and biases in the brain: Dual neural pathways for decision making. In O. Vartanian and D. R. Mandel (Eds.), *Neuroscience of decision-making* (125–142). New York, NY: Psychology Press.

De Neys, W. and Van Gelder, E. (2009). Logic and belief across the lifespan: the rise and fall of belief inhibition during syllogistic reasoning. *Developmental Science, 12,* 123–130.

De Neys, W., Vartanian, O. and Goel, V. (2008). Smarter than we think: When our brains detect that we are biased. *Psychological Science, 19,* 483–489.

Dunning, D. (1999). A newer look: Motivated social cognition and the schematic representation of social concepts. *Psychological Inquiry,* 10, 1–11.

Epstein, S. (1990). Cognitive experiential self theory. In L. Pervin (Ed.), *Handbook of personality: Theory and research* (pp. 165–192). New York, NY: Guilford Press.

Epstein, S. (1994). Integration of the cognitive and psychodynamic unconscious. *American Psychologist, 49,* 709–724.

Epstein, S. (2003). Cognitive-experiential self-theory of personality. In T. Millon and Lerner, J. Melvin (Eds.), *Handbook of psychology: Personality and social psychology* (Vol. 5., pp. 159–184). Hoboken, NJ: John Wiley and Sons Inc.

Epstein, S., Pacini, R., Denes-Raj, V. and Heier, H. (1996). Individual differences in intuitive-experiential and analytical-rational thinking styles. *Journal of Personality and Social Psychology, 71,* 390–405.

Evans, J. St B. T. (1984). Heuristic and analytic processing in reasoning. *British Journal of Psychology, 75,* 451–468.

Evans, J. S. B.T. (2003). In two minds: Dual process accounts of reasoning. *Trends in Cognitive Sciences, 7,* 454–459.

Evans, J. S. B. T. and Over, D. E. (1996). *Rationality and reasoning.* Psychology Press.

Evans, J. S. B. T., Barston, J. L. and Pollard, P. (1983). On the conflict between logic and belief in syllogistic reasoning. *Memory and Cognition, 11,* 295–306.

Forstmann, B. U., Jahfari, S., Scholte, H. S., Wolfensteller, U., van den Wildenberg, W. P. and Ridderinkhof, K. R. (2008). Function and structure of the right inferior frontal cortex predict individual differences in response inhibition: A model-based approach. *The Journal of Neuroscience*, *28*, 9790–9796.

Goffman, E. (1959/2002). *The presentation of self in everyday life*. Garden City, NY: Anchor.

Greenwald, A. G. and Farnham, S. D. (2000). Using the implicit association test to measure self-esteem and self-concept. *Journal of Personality and Social Psychology*, *79*, 1022–1038.

Han, S. and Northoff, G. (2008). Culture-sensitive neural substrates of human cognition: A transcultural neuroimaging approach. *Nature Reviews Neuroscience*, *9*, 646–654.

Hannover, B. and K{umlaut u}hnen, U. (2009). Culture and social cognition in human interaction. In F. Strack and J. Förster (Eds.), *Social cognition. The basis of human interaction* (pp. 291–309). London: Taylor & Francis / Psychology Press.

Hannover, B., Pöhlmann, C., Springer, A. and Röder, U. (2005). Implications of independent versus interdependent self-knowledge for motivated social cognition: The Semantic Procedural Interface Model of the Self. *Self and Identity*, *5*, 159–175.

Houdé, O. (2007). First insights on ''neuropedagogy of reasoning''. *Thinking and Reasoning*, *13*, 81–89.

Inbar, Y., Cone, J. and Gilovich, T. (2010). People's intuitions about intuitive insight and intuitive choice. *Journal of Personality and Social Psychology*, *99*, 232–247.

Kahneman, D. and Frederick, S. (2002) Representativeness revisited: Attribute substitution in intuitive judgment. In T. Gilovich, D. Griffin and D. Kahneman (Eds.), *Heuristics and biases: The psychology of intuitive judgment* (pp. 49–81). Cambridge, UK: Cambridge University Press.

Kahneman, D. and Frederick, S. (2005) A model of heuristic judgment. In K. J. Holyoak and R. G. Morris (Eds.), *The Cambridge Handbook of Thinking and Reasoning* (pp. 267–93). Cambridge, UK: Cambridge University Press.

Kahneman, D. and Tversky, A. (1973). On the psychology of prediction. *Psychological Review*, *80*, 237–251.

Kahneman, D., Slovic, P. and Tversky, A. (1982). *Judgement under uncertainty: Heuristics and biases*. Cambridge, MA: Cambridge University Press.

Kim, K., Grimm, L. R. and Markman, A. B. (2007). Self-construal and the processing of covariation information in causal reasoning. *Memory and Cognition*, *35*, 1337–1343.

Klaczynski, P. A., Gordon, D. H. and Fauth, J. (1997). Goal-oriented critical reasoning and individual differences in critical reasoning biases. *Journal of Educational Psychology*, *89* (3), 470.

Kühnen, U. and Oyserman, D. (2002). Thinking about the self influences thinking in general: Cognitive consequences of salient self-concept. *Journal of Experimental Social Psychology*, *38*, 492–499.

Kühnen, U., Hannover, B. and Schubert, B. (2001). The Semantic-Procedural-Interface model of the self: The role of self-knowledge for context-dependent versus context-independent modes of thinking. *Journal of Personality and Social Psychology*, *80*, 397–409.

Kunda, Z. (1987). Motivated inference: Self-serving generation and evaluation of causal theories. *Journal of Personality and Social Psychology*, 53, 636–647.

Kunda, Z. (1990). The case for motivated reasoning. *Psychological Bulletin*, *108*, 480–498.

Kunda, Z. and Sanitioso, R. (1989). Motivated changes in the self-concept. *Journal of Experimental Social Psychology*, *25*, 272–285.

Lin, Z. and Han, S. (2009). Self-construal priming modulates the scope of visual attention. *The Quarterly Journal of Experimental Psychology, 62*, 802–813.

Lin, Z., Lin, J. and Han, S. (2008). Self-construal priming modulates visual activity underlying global/local perception. *Biological Psychology, 77*, 93–97.

Markus, H. R. (1977). Self-schemata and processing information about the self. *Journal of Personality and Social Psychology, 35*, 63–78.

Markus, H. R. and Kitayama, S. (1991). Culture and the self: Implications for cognition, emotion, and motivation. *Psychological Review, 98*, 224–253.

Markus, H. and Kunda, Z. (1986). Stability and malleability of self-concept. *Journal of Personality and Social Psychology, 51*, 858–866.

Markus, H. and Nurius, P. (1986). Possible selves. *American Psychologist, 41*, 954–969.

Markus, H. and Ruvolo, A. (1989). Possible selves: Personalized representations of goals. In L. A. Pervin (Ed.), *Goal concepts in personality and social psychology* (pp. 211–242). Hillsdale, NJ: Erlbaum.

Markus, H. and Wurf, E. (1987). The dynamic self-concept: A social psychological perspective. *Annual Review of Psychology, 38*, 299–337.

Moutier, S. and Houdé, O. (2003). Judgment under uncertainty and conjunction fallacy inhibition training. *Thinking and Reasoning, 9*, 185–201.

Osman, M. (2004). An evaluation of dual-process theories of reasoning. *Psychonomic Bulletin and Review, 11*, 988–1010.

Osman, M. (2007). Can tutoring improve performance on a reasoning task under deadline conditions? *Memory and cognition, 35*, 342–351.

Oyserman, D. and Lee, S. (2008). Does culture influence what and how we think? Effects of priming individualism and collectivism. *Psychological Bulletin, 34*, 311–342.

Oyserman, D. and Sorensen, N. (2009). Understanding cultural syndrome effects on what and how we think: A situated cognition model. In C. Chiu, R. Wyer Jr. and Y. Hong (Eds.), *Problems and solutions in cross-cultural theory, research and application* (pp. 25–52). New York, NY: Psychology Press.

Oyserman, D., Coon, H. M. and Kemmelmeier, M. (2002). Rethinking individualism and collectivism: Evaluation of theoretical assumptions and meta-analyses. *Psychological Bulletin, 128*, 3–72.

Pacini, R. and Epstein, S. (1999). The relation of rational and experiential information processing styles to personality, basic beliefs, and the ratio-bias phenomenon. *Journal of Personality and Social Psychology, 76*, 972–987.

Pacini, R., Muir, F. and Epstein, S. (1998). Depressive realism from the perspective of cognitive-experiential self-theory. *Journal of Personality and Social Psychology, 74*, 1056–1068.

Peters, K. R. and Gawronski, B. (2011). Are we puppets on a string? Comparing the impact of contingency and validity on implicit and explicit evaluations. *Personality and Social Psychology Bulletin, 37*, 557–569.

Pyszczynski, T. and Greenberg, J. (1987). Toward an integration of cognitive and motivational perspectives on social inference: A biased hypothesis-testing model. In L. Berkowitz, *Advances in experimental social psychology* (Vol. 20, pp. 297–340). San Diego, CA: Academic Press.

Reyna, V.F. and Farley, F. (2006). Risk and rationality in adolescent decision making: Implications for theory, practice, and public policy. *Psychological Science in the Public Interest*, 7 (1), 1–44.

Sá, W., West, R.F. and Stanovich, K.E. (1999). The domain specificity and generality of belief bias: searching for a generalizable critical thinking skill. *Journal of Educational Psychology, 91*, 497–510.

Sanitioso, R. (1998). Behavioural consequences of motivated self-concept change. *European Journal of Social Psychology, 28*, 281–285.

Sanitioso, R. (2008). Motivated self and recall: visual perspectives in remembering past behaviors. *European Journal of Social Psychology, 38*, 566–575.

Sanitioso, R. and Niedenthal, P. M. (2006). Ease of recall and motivated self-perception. *Self and Identity*, 5, 73–84.

Sanitioso, R. and Wlodarski, R. (2004). In search of information that confirms a desired self- perception: Motivated processing of social feedback and choice of social interactions. *Personality and Social Psychology Bulletin, 30*, 412–422.

Sanitioso, R., Conway, M. A. and Brunot, S. (2006). Autobiographical memories, the self and comparison processes. In S. Guimond (Ed.), *Social comparison and social psychology: Understanding cognition, intergroup relation and culture*. Cambridge, UK: Cambridge University Press.

Sanitioso, R., Kunda, Z. and Fong, G. T. (1990). Motivated recruitment of autobiographical memories. *Journal of Personality and Social Psychology, 59*, 229–241.

Schlenker, B. R. (1980). *Impression management: The self-concept, social identity, and interpersonal relations*. Monterey, CA: Brooks/Cole Publishing Company.

Shiloh, S., Salton, E. and Sharabi, D. (2002). Individual differences in rational and intuitive thinking styles as predictors of heuristic responses and framing effects. *Personality and Individual Differences, 32*, 415–429.

Sloman, S. A. (1996). The empirical case for two systems of reasoning. *Psychological Bulletin, 119*, 3–22.

Springer, A., Beyer, J., Derrfuss, J., Volz, K.G. and Hannover, B. (2012). Seeing you or the scene? Self-construals modulate inhibitory mechanisms of attention. *Social Cognition, 30*, 133–152.

Stanovich, K. E. and West, R. F. (2000) Individual differences in reasoning: Implications for the rationality debate. *Behavioral and Brain Sciences, 23*, 645–726.

Steinberg, L. (2004). Risk taking in adolescence: What changes, and why? *Annals of the New York Academy of Sciences, 1021*, 51–58.

Steinberg, L. (2007). Risk taking in adolescence: New perspectives from brain and behavior science. *Current Directions in Psychological Science, 16*, 55–59.

Swann, W. B., Jr. and Bosson, J. (2010). Self and identity. In S. T. Fiske, D. T. Gilbert and G. Lindzey (Eds.), *Handbook of social psychology* (5th ed., pp. 589–628). New York, NY: McGraw-Hill.

Swann Jr, W. B., Bosson, J. K. and Pelham, B. W. (2002). Different partners, different selves: Strategic verification of circumscribed identities. *Personality and Social Psychology Bulletin, 28*, 1215–1228.

Taylor, S. E. and Brown, J. D. (1988). Illusion and well-being: A social psychological perspective on mental health. *Psychological Bulletin, 103*, 193–210.

Vogeley, K. and Roepstorff, A. (2009). Contextualizing culture and social cognition. *Trends in Cognitive Sciences, 13*, 511–516.

Witteman, C., van den Bercken, J., Claes, L. and Godoy, A. (2009). Assessing rational and intuitive thinking styles. *European Journal of Psychological Assessment, 25*, 39–47.

7 Probabilistic reasoning

Rational expectations in young children and infants

Vittorio Girotto

Introduction

Are naïve individuals, namely, those who have not mastered the probability calculus, able to reason correctly about probabilities? In particular, are young children able to form correct expectations about uncertain events? Posing questions of this sort challenges some influential views of probabilistic reasoning according to which individuals are unable to deal with uncertainty, unless they have received some kind of formal education on probability and statistics. This chapter discusses a recent series of studies that have taken such a challenge seriously and provided evidence against those views.

The chapter starts with an illustration of the difficulties intelligent adults have in solving elementary probabilistic problems, and with a brief discussion of their possible sources. Then, it presents the hypothesis according to which naïve individuals can correctly infer the probability of an event without explicitly applying the formal rules of the probability calculus. Rather than applying these rules, such individuals intuitively evaluate chance by considering the various possibilities in which an event may or may not occur. The central part of the chapter reviews the main source of evidence in favour of this hypothesis: the finding that even young children can correctly infer the probability of an event by reasoning about the possibilities in which it may occur. The final part of the chapter discusses the thesis according to which only formal instruction allows individuals to assess chance, and boldly claims that all human beings possess a correct intuition of probability, regardless of their education and cultural background.

Alternative views of probabilistic reasoning

In a masterly series of studies, Kahneman and Tversky have shown that untutored individuals make judgments that do not always respect the elementary rules of mathematical probability (e.g., Kahneman, Slovic and Tversky, 1982). For example, practicing physicians judged that a patient who had pulmonary embolism more likely experienced "dyspnea and hemiparesis" than "hemiparesis" (Tversky and Kahneman, 1983). Their judgment violated the conjunction rule of the probability calculus, which dictates that a conjunction cannot be more likely than one of its constituents. Individuals commit this error when, for example, one constituent (e.g., dyspnea) but not the other (e.g., hemiparesis) is *representative* of a given condition (e.g., having had a pulmonary embolism). Evaluating the probability of an event on the basis of its representativeness illustrates the intuitive procedures (aka *heuristics*) that often govern probabilistic reasoning.

The discovery that adult evaluations may violate basic rules of probability has stimulated a lively debate about the nature of human reasoning. In particular, some authors have claimed that failure to solve Kahneman and Tversky's problems does not prove that naïve individuals err due to their application of inappropriate heuristics (e.g., Cosmides and Tooby, 1996; Gigerenzer and Hoffrage, 1995). According to these authors, the human mind is blind to the probability of single events, and it is able to reason probabilistically only about frequencies of multiple, repeatable events. Therefore, naïve individuals fail problems like those devised by Kahneman and Tversky's because they ask for the evaluation of a single event (e.g., the probability that a given patient presents some symptoms). By contrast, the same individuals can solve versions of these problems that present information in the form of frequencies of observations, and ask for a frequency estimation. For example, individuals do not violate the conjunction rule when they tackle problems like the following one (adapted from Tversky and Kahneman, 1983):

> A health survey was conducted in a sample of 100 adult males in British Columbia, of all ages and occupations. Please give your best estimate of the following values:
>
> How many of the 100 participants have had one or more heart attacks?
>
> How many of the 100 participants are both over 55 years olds and have had one or more heart attacks?

The problem asks for an assessment of frequency. Respondents correclty assign a lower estimate to the second question than to the first, and so they conform to the conjunction rule.

It is debatable whether the human mind is actually tuned to natural occurring frequencies, which is a claim made to explain why frequency problems are often easier than single-case probability problems (Girotto and Gonzalez, 2001, 2002; Hoffrage, Gigerenzer, Krauss and Martignon, 2002). Even more debatable, as we will see shortly, is the claim that naïve individuals are incapbable of reasoning about the probability of single events. Consider the following problem:

> There is a transparent container in which there are three identical objects, and a single other object which differs from the rest according to shape and colour. All of the objects bounce around randomly. After some time, the container is covered and one object exits from an opening at the base of the container. You do not see the shape or the colour of the object. Which is the more probable outcome: that the object that exited from the opening is one of the three identical objects, or that it is the singleton?

The question asks for a single-event evaluation. Yet, you are likely to answer: "One of the three identical objects". Your answer is normatively correct. It agrees with a basic principle of classical probability that states that the probability of an event equals the proportion of possibilities in which it occurs. Simple evaluations of this sort indicate that the human mind can deal with the probability of single events. Your answer exemplifies a common and simple way to reason about uncertainty, which has been defined *extensional reasoning* (Johnson-Laird, Legrenzi, Girotto, Sonino-Legrenzi and Caverni, 1999). It consists of assessing the chances of an event by considering and counting the different ways in which it can occur. In this case, if you assign the same probability of exiting to each single object, you may easily judge that the object that exits from the opening is more likely to belong to the class with three instances, because there are three possibilities in favour of this hypothesis and only one possibility in favour of the alternative one. This intuitive grasp of probabilities is based on elementary skills that children appear to possess early in their development. In particular, young children are able to compare quantities (e.g., Barth, Le Mont, Lipton and Spelke, 2005), so therefore, young children should be able to compare chances, even if they are not able to express chances numerically. The studies reviewed in the next sections have tested and corroborated such a crucial prediction of the extensional reasoning hypothesis. Moreover, these findings present an fundamental challenge to claims that humans in general are unable to reason accurately about single-case probabilities.

Correct reasoning about chances in young children

How do children reason about probability? As it is often the case for issues concerning the development of human reasoning, Piaget was the first to address such a question (Piaget, 1950; Piaget and Inhelder, 1951/1975). The basic assumption of the Piagetian theory is that there is a parallel development of logical and probabilistic reasoning. Accordingly, young children cannot reason correctly about probability because they lack the basic logical abilities to do so. In particular, before the age of about seven children do not master the part–whole logical relation. Let us take the following example to illustrate. Suppose you present five- or six-year-olds a bag containing four apples and two pears, and ask them whether there are more apples or more fruits in the bag. They will answer that there are more apples in the bag. Following the Piagetian explanation, young children fail because they treat the question as if it asked for a comparison of the two subsets (apples vs. pears), rather than for a subset-superordinate set comparison (see Piaget and Szeminska, 1941/1952). One relevant consequence of this logical deficit is that young children should fail problems whose solution requires them to take into account probability ratios, that is, to relate the number of favourable possibilities to the total number of possibilities. Indeed, Piaget and Inhelder (1951/1975) reported observations according to which six-year-olds failed problems like the following one:

> Look at these chips [The experimenter points at a bag containing one red chip and three white chips]. If you take one of these chips from the bag without looking, do you think that it is easier to get a red or a white chip?

Children answered "A red chip", and so they apparently supported Piaget and Inhelder's claim: Young children focus on one possibility (e.g., I draw the red chip), while neglecting its relation to the ensemble of all possibilities (e.g., I draw one of these four chips). Notice that this problem did not ask children to make an *absolute* probability evaluation (i.e., "What is the probability of getting a red chip?"), but a comparative one ("Is it easier to get a red or a white chip?"). To answer the latter question correctly, children did not need to compute a probability ratio. They simply needed to compare the two subsets of chips (three white vs. one red). Children possess the ability to do so. Indeed, following the Piagetian explanation, they fail to solve part–whole problems precisely because they make a comparison of the two subsets (four apples vs. two pears), rather than a subset–superordinate set comparison (four apples vs. six fruits). Thus, children's failure to solve elementary probability problems of this sort is surprising, even in the light of Piaget and Inhelder's hypothesis.

Piaget's work had many merits. It was the first to investigate children's probabilistic reasoning and to provide a general account of the development of probabilistic cognition. The reliability of the results reported in Piaget's studies, however, is questionable. Subsequent studies, which have employed more controlled experimental conditions, showed that young children are able to solve problems asking them to make a relative probability evaluation (e.g., Brainerd, 1981; Davis, 1965; Goldberg, 1966) or to choose the more likely of two outcomes (e.g., Yost, Siegel and Andrews, 1962). For example, five-year-olds are able to solve problems like the following one (adapted from Brainerd, 1981):

> Look at these animals. [The experimenter shows seven chips representing monkeys and three chips representing birds.] I'm going to put all these chips in this bag. [The experimenter puts the chips in an opaque bag.] I shake the bag, so that I mix the monkeys and the birds up. If I close my eyes and take one chip from the container, do you think I will get a monkey or a bird?

Most children correctly answer "A monkey". They are particularly likely to do so when they are initially required to compare the size of the two sets. For example, most children who have to indicate whether there are more monkeys or more birds in the bag answer "More monkeys". All of those who produce this answer make the correct prediction that the experimenter is more likely to get a monkey from the bag. In sum, young children do well in probability problems whose solution implies a simple comparison of two subsets of possibilities (e.g., monkeys vs. birds).

These results are important, despite the fact that they have been neglected in the literature on adult probabilistic reasoning. They contradict Piaget and Inhelder's hypothesis, and corroborate the extensional reasoning one: Even pre-school children make predictions based on a correct evaluation of possibilities. These results, however, concern elementary situations, in which the occurrence of an outcome (e.g., drawing a chip from a bag) only depends on the initial distribution of a population (e.g., the proportion of the chip colours in the bag). Could children solve problems that ask them to consider more specific information about the outcome's process (e.g., the shape of a chip drawn from the bag)? In other words, are children's probabilistic intuitions confined to the evaluation of *prior* probability or do they extend to *posterior* probability? The studies reviewed in the following section have addressed such questions by challenging the common view that evaluating posterior probability is at the fringes of human competence (Johnson-Laird, 2006).

Children's evaluation of posterior probability

Consider the following problem (adapted from Girotto and Gonzalez, 2008/Experiment 2):

> Look at these chips. [The experimenter shows four round and four square chips. All the round chips are black. Three of the square chips are white and one is black.] I'm going to put all these chips in this bag, but you can remember how they are because they are copied in this card. [The experimenter puts the chips in an opaque bag, and places the card depicting the eight chips in front of the child.] I'll shake the bag, and I'll take one chip from it, without looking. Before I take it, you have to answer my question: Do you think I will take a black or a white chip? If your answer turns out to be right, you'll win a piece of candy.

From the age of five, children answer "A black chip". Their answer is correct and confirms the previous finding that pre-schoolers are able to assess prior probability (e.g., Brainerd, 1981). Are they also able to assess posterior probability? In other words, are pre-schoolers able to integrate general information about the prior set of possibilities and new information about a specific event? Let us consider what this means using the following example. Suppose that the experimenter takes one chip, keeps it in her hand and says:

> Ah, listen. I'm touching the chip that I have taken and now I know something that might help you to win the game. I'm touching the chip that I have in my hand and I feel that it is square. Do you think that it is a black or a white chip?

The new piece of information modifies the set of possibilities one needs to consider. To answer correctly, one has to focus on the subset of possibilities compatible with the evidence (i.e., the four squares). Posterior information, however, asks for the same extensional treatment as prior information does, that is, comparing the possibilities of the alternative outcomes (i.e., three white squares vs. one black square). Children should be able to do so, on the condition that they are able to integrate information they receive from different sources. Indeed, by the age of five, children are able to integrate pieces of information received from two successive messages and, if it is the case, to modify their initial interpretation (Beck and Robinson, 2001). Therefore, children of this age should be able to integrate prior and posterior information and, if it is the case, to revise their initial evaluation. For example, given the specific information that the taken chip is square, they should answer "white", updating their initial judgement. A series of studies conducted by Girotto and Gonzalez (2008) showed that this is the case: From the age of five, children correctly integrate prior and posterior information and revise their judgments and choices in the light of new evidence.

You might have noticed that in the previous problems children reasoned about the random outcome of a change device, namely, the drawing of a chip from a bag. Events of this sort are repeatable. One might also ask, could children reason correctly about non-repeatable events? This question is theoretically relevant, given that the frequentist hypothesis posits that the human mind is able to reason probabilistically, but only about frequencies of repeatable events (Cosmides and Tooby, 1996; Gigerenzer and Hoffrage, 1995). Consider the following problem (adapted from Girotto and Gonzalez, 2008/Experiment 3):

> Look at these animal toys. They live in these two houses. [The experimenter points at two boxes.] Some live in this house. [The experimenter points at a box containing two cats and one dog.] Some others live in this house. [The experimenter points at a box containing one cat and two dogs.] While the animals were outside, a troll put one chocolate in the bag of one of the animals. In the evening, the animals went home without checking what they had in their bags. Thus, now there is a chocolate in one house, but nobody knows in which one. Only the troll knows, and he has written it in a letter that he has put in this sealed envelope. [The experimenter shows a sealed envelope] If you find the animal that has the bag with the chocolate, you win the chocolate. You can choose one of the two houses in order to find the animal that has the bag with the chocolate. Which house do you choose?

In this case, no cue favours one house over the other, because they contain the same number of animal toys (i.e., three). Moreover, it is difficult to associate a specific kind of animal with the chocolate, which, in any event, has been secretly placed by the troll and not deliberately taken by one of the animals. Thus, children should choose one of the two houses at random. Assume that they do so. Then, the experimenter silently reads the troll's letter and asks them:

> In this letter, the troll has written what kind of animal is carrying the chocolate. Do you want to know which kind of animal this is?

Of course, children are eager to receive this piece of information. Suppose that the experimenter informs them that a dog carries the chocolate. In this case, the specific information does favour one of the two houses: The house with two dogs has twice as many chances of containing the animal with the chocolate than the house with only one dog. Following the Piagetian account (Piaget and Inhelder, 1951/1975), children should focus on one possibility (i.e., one dog carries the chocolate), and neglect its relation to the entire set of possibilities (i.e., there are three dogs, each of them could be carrying the chocolate). Accordingly, they should erroneously select the house with only one dog. In addition, following the frequentist hypothesis, individuals are unable to reason about single events (Cosmides and Tooby, 1996; Gigerenzer and Hoffrage, 1995). Therefore, children should fail this sort of task, because it asks them to consider a single, not repeatable outcome, produced by an intentional agent. Consequently, children should randomly select one of the two houses. By contrast, following the extensional reasoning hypothesis, children should answer correctly, by means of a simple comparison of two sets of possibilities. In particular, children who have randomly chosen the house with only one dog should be able to switch to the one with two dogs. The results obtained by Girotto and Gonzalez (2008/Experiment 3) have corroborated the extensional reasoning hypothesis: From the age of five, children, including those who have originally make the wrong choice, select the house favoured by the new piece of evidence, namely, the one with two dogs. In sum, they are able to revise their choices concerning a single, non-repeatable event, in the light of posterior evidence.

Children's evaluation of the probability of a relation

The results presented so far corroborate the naïve extensional view, showing that even young children can form correct expectations about uncertain events. In the described studies, however, the events were characterized by a *simple property*, like the colour of a chip. For example, in order to judge whether it is more likely that a yellow chip or a blue chip is drawn from a box, you need to consider just the colour of the chips: The higher the proportion of chips of a given colour, the greater the probability of drawing a chip of that colour. The open question, then, is to establish whether naïve individuals, in particular children, are able to make correct probability judgments when the possibilities they have to evaluate concern *relations between simple properties*. In other words, the open question is: Do children form appropriate expectations when they have to mentally combine possibilities?

Even in response to this question, Piaget was the first to provide an answer. In a study that can be considered the very first empirical work on probabilistic reasoning, Piaget (1950) presented preschoolers and school children with a series of problems designed to test their predictions about a relation. One of these problems read as follows:

> Look at these chips. [The experimenter shows a series of chips ordered by colour and number: one pink, two red, three green, four blue, five yellow, six white.] We leave these chips on the table so that you can look at them, and we put these other chips in a bag. [The experimenter puts a series of chips identical to those presented on the table in an opaque bag.] If you take two of these chips from the bag without looking, which colours are easier to get?

Both preschoolers and school children failed to provide a correct answer to Piaget's question. According to Piaget (see also Piaget and Inhelder, 1951/1975), their failure demonstrates that they lacked the logical abilities necessary to combine possibilities in a systematic way. Only when individuals reach the final stage of cognitive development, which takes place during adolescence, do they acquire such abilities, and can therefore solve problems that ask for a combinatorial treatment of possibilities. Followers of Piaget apparently confirmed and aggravated his pessimistic view: They showed that only formal instruction allows adolescents to acquire the basic notions of combinatorics, and to use them appropriately in tackling probability problems (Fischbein, 1975; Fischbein and Schnarch, 1997).

The results reported by Piaget and his followers are open to question. Does the finding that children are unable to solve problems like the above-described one really demonstrate that they are unable to reason about the possibilities of a relation? In fact, the Piagetian problem asks to predict one *specific* result, namely, the colour of two chips randomly taken from the bag. In order to answer correctly, you have to consider the entire set of outcomes, that is, the twenty possible combinations of colours that you can get by randomly taking two chips from the back. Then, you have to count and compare the possibilities favouring each outcome. Moreover, the problem asks you to predict a very unlikely outcome. Indeed, the most likely outcome, namely, taking one white chip and one yellow chip, has less than a 15 per cent chance of occurring. In sum, the problems used by Piaget and his followers present some specific requirements that may have concealed children's abilities to reason correctly about the probably of a relation between simple properties. Thus, if one wants to examine whether such abilities really exist, one has to devise novel and more appropriate experimental paradigms.

Consider the following problem (adapted from Gonzalez and Girotto, 2011/ Experiment 1):

> Look at these chips. [The experimenter shows two red chips, two green chips, two blue chips, and two yellow chips.] I'm going to put all these chips in this bag, but you can remember how they are because they are copied in this card. [The experimenter puts the chips in an opaque bag, and leaves the card depicting the eight chips in front of the child.] I'll shake the bag, and you'll take two chips from it at the same time, without looking. Before you take them, you have to answer my question: Do you think you will take two chips of two different colours or two chips of the same colour? If your answer turns out to be right, you'll win a piece of candy.

If you possess the logical abilities that Piaget attributed to adult reasoning, you should answer by considering all the possible pairs of chips, and the resulting combinations of colours. In this way, you will conclude that it is more likely to take two chips of two different colours, because there are just four pairs of chips of the same colour and 24 pairs of chips of two different colours. There is, however, an alternative way to reach such a conclusion. Indeed, you might consider only a *sample* of all the possible outcomes. For example, you might consider just one chip, and note that many chips of different colours surround it. Thus, you might conclude that it is more likely to get two chips of two different colours, because for each chip there is only one chip having the same colour, and many more chips having a different colour. This conclusion is the same as the one you might draw by applying a systematic treatment of possibilities. In both cases, the probability of getting two chips of two different colours is six times greater than the probability of getting two chips of the same colour. The new conclusion, however, is based on an *approximate comparison* of possibilities, namely, those in which a given relation occurs (i.e., "Two chips of the same colour") and those in which it does not (i.e., "Two chips of two different colours"). The simpler nature of such a treatment of possibilities should allow children to arrive at the same, correct conclusion. Indeed, unlike the traditional Piagetian problem, the novel one does not ask to predict a specific outcome (i.e., "Which is the more likely pair of colours?"). Rather, it asks to predict whether a given relation (i.e., "The two chips will have the same colour") is more likely to occur or not to occur. As we have seen in the previous sections, children are able to make approximate comparisons of possibilities. Therefore, they should be able to solve the novel problem by applying a simplified treatment of possibilities like the one described above. Notice, moreover, that the correct solution of the novel problem consists in predicting an outcome that has at least a 50 per cent chance of occurring. In sum, the novel problem does not present the limits of the traditional Piagetian tasks and so children should be more likely to solve them. This prediction has been tested and corroborated in a series of studies in which children aged five to ten had to predict the "same colour" relation between two chips randomly taken from a bag (Gonzalez and Girotto, 2011). By the age of six, children made correct judgments about the probability of such a relation, and that by the age of nine, their performance reached adult level.

These results are at odds with those reported in previous studies. However, they could be attributed to the application of some superficial, non-combinatorial heuristic. For example, children might have judged that the pair was more likely to contain two chips of two different colours because in the bag there was a variety of colours. In other words, children might have simply considered the *colour distribution* in the set of chips, rather than the *colour relation* between pairs of chips. To test this possibility one has to devise problems whose solution cannot be reached without taking into account the relation between two elements. Consider the following problem (adapted from Gonzalez and Girotto, 2011/Experiment 2):

> Look at this cardboard. [The experimenter shows the cardboard depicted in Figure 7.1.] It is a triangle drawn inside a rectangle. The rectangle is divided in strips. I'm going to put all these strips in this bag, but you can remember how they are because they are copied on this cardboard. [The experimenter puts the strips in an opaque bag, and places the cardboard depicting the ten strips in front of the child.] I'll shake the bag, and you'll take two strips from it at the same time, without looking. Before you take them, you have to answer my question: Do you think you will take two strips that touch each other or two strips that do not touch each other? If your answer turns out to be right, you'll win a piece of candy.

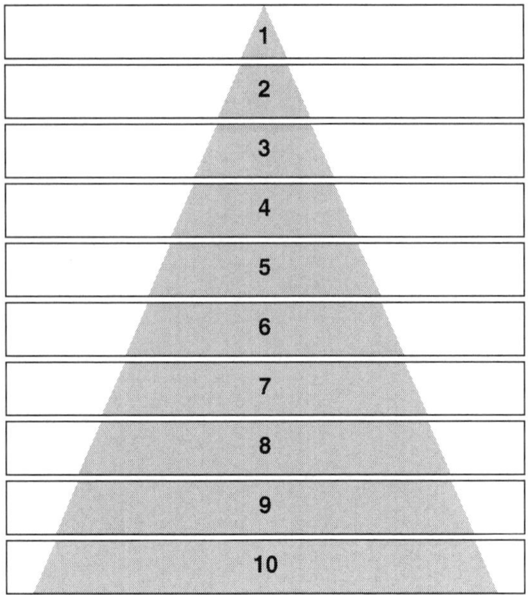

Figure 7.1 Example of the materials used by Gonzalez and Girotto (2011).

To answer correctly, you do not need to make a precise evaluation of the proportion of possibilities in which the relation "touch each other" holds. You might simply focus on a sample of these possibilities and then compare those favouring the hypothesis "the two strips touch each other" with those favouring the hypothesis "the two strips do not touch each other". For example, if you focus on any of the central strips (e.g., strip number 5), you might note that it touches two strips (e.g., strips number 4 and number 6), and it does not touch many other strips. Accordingly, you might conclude that it is more likely that you get two strips which do not touch each other, without making a precise counting. Indeed, the higher the number of strips you cut in the triangle, the greater the number of strips that do not touch each other. In sum, like in the chip problem, you might produce a correct evaluation by means of a simplified treatment of possibilities. Unlike the chip problem, however, you cannot solve the triangle problem without taking into account a relation between two tokens. Indeed, unlike the colour, "touching" is not an inherent property of a single token. Therefore, if children can solve this sort of problem correctly, one can conclude that they are actually able to reason about the probability of a relation. The results obtained by Gonzalez and Girotto (2011/ Experiments 2 and 3) have corroborated this prediction: From the age of seven, children make correct predictions about the occurrence of the touching relation, namely, a relation that does not depend on the distribution of simple properties among the tokens. In sum, school children correctly apply their elementary combinatorial abilities to solve probability problems.

Taken together, the results discussed in this section suggest that children's probabilistic intuitions emerge at the age of about six. Could these results be taken to imply that schooling shapes probabilistic cognition? The answer to this question is considered in the next section.

Infants' probabilistic intuitions

Various pieces of evidence suggest that schooling does not determine the ability to draw elementary probabilistic inferences. In fact, children appear to be able to assess prior (e.g., Brainerd, 1981) and posterior (Girotto and Gonzalez, 2008) probability before starting school. Moreover, the arithmetical skills they need to do so appear to be independent of schooling: Even preschoolers (e.g., Barth et al., 2005) and individuals living in illiterate cultures (e.g., Pica, Lerner, Izard and Dehaene, 2004) are able to compare and add quantities. The most telling evidence, however, has been produced by the recent discovery that even preverbal or barely verbal infants have some probabilistic intuitions.

One of the most widely used techniques to study infant cognition consists in measuring how long infants look at a given event. Their looking time may be considered as an index of surprise: The more unexpected the event, the longer infants look at it. Looking-time studies have shown that infants have expectations about novel events based on object numerosity (e.g., Wynn, 1992), other individual's goals (e.g., Surian, Caldi and Sperber, 2007), and physical cues (e.g., Spelke, 1990). Therefore, if infants form probabilistic expectations about future outcomes, they should look longer at unlikely events than at likely ones. To test such a prediction, a group of 12-month-olds was presented with a video in which three identical objects and one different in shape and colour bounced randomly in a transparent container, similar to the one described in the first section of this chapter (Teglas, Girotto, Gonzalez and Bonatti, 2007/Experiment 1). After some time, the container was covered and one object exited from an opening at the base. In some cases the singleton exited from the opening, in others, one of the three identical objects did. If infants did not possess any probabilistic intuitions, their reactions would have been the same in both cases. Instead, infants looked reliably longer at the scene when the singleton, rather than one of the three identical objects, exited from the opening. The infants' reactions indicate that from early in their development individuals possess some probabilistic intuitions. Their reactions, however, could also be attributed to some non-probabilistic heuristics. For instance, their reactions would mean that infants look longer at the scene when the singleton exits not because it is the less likely event, but because it is the perceptually most salient one. To rule out this alternative interpretation, a group of 12-month-olds was presented with a video showing the same container as the previously described one, with the exception that the three identical objects could not exit because they were confined in the top part of the container by a separator in the middle of it. After the occlusion time, that is, the period in which the container was covered, one object, either the singleton or else one of the three identical objects, exited from the opening. Notice that objects and outcomes were the same as in the previous experiment. However, the presence of the separator transformed the more probable event of the previous experiment, namely, the exit of one of the three identical objects, into an impossible event, and the less improbable event of the previous experiment, namely, the exit of the singleton, into the only possible one. If infants' reactions depended on a tendency to focus on the perceptually most salient outcome, then they would have looked longer at the scene when the singleton exited, even if it was the only possible event. Instead, if infants' reactions depended on the different probabilities of the events, then they would have looked longer at the scene when one of the three identical objects exited, because it was an impossible event. The results reported by Teglas et al. (2007/Experiment 2) corroborated the latter prediction: Infants looked reliably longer at the impossible event than at the possible one, showing that they reacted rationally at the probabilities and possibilities of the events, rather than to simple perceptual factors. The results obtained with looking-time methodology have been replicated in a task that required infants to make a choice. When 12- to 14-month-old infants are encouraged to walk or crawl to one of two cups in order to get a reward, they tend to choose the cup that is more likely to contain it (Denison and Xu, 2010).

Finally, recent results have shown that infants possess sophisticated abilities to integrate different sources of information when they form expectations about future events (Teglas, Vul, Girotto, Gonzalez, Tenenbaum and Bonatti, 2011). Consider, once again, the above-described container, in its original form, namely, without the separator. Suppose you use a very short occlusion time (i.e., 0.04 second): How would infants react? If, before occlusion, the three identical objects were near the opening and the singleton far from it, they will look longer at the exit of the singleton, just as they did in Teglas et al.'s (2007/Experiment 1) study. But what if, before occlusion, the singleton was near the opening and the three identical objects far from it? If infants' reactions are shaped only by the number of objects of each class in the scene, then infants should look longer at the exit of the singleton, because it belongs to the less numerous class. By contrast, if infants form expectations based on both the number of objects in each class and their spatial arrangement, then they should look longer at the exit of one of the identical objects, because they were far from the opening at the moment of the occlusion. The results obtained by Teglas et al. (2011) have corroborated the latter prediction, showing that 12-month-olds anticipated the exit of an object close to the opening, disregarding the number of objects in each class. This finding supports the hypothesis that infants form expectations about future events by integrating numerical and spatial cues, and provides further evidence against the hypothesis that their different reactions depend on the perceptual salience of the singleton. Indeed, infants looked shorter at its exit than at the exit of one the identical objects when, before occlusion, the singleton was close to the opening. In other words, they looked shorter at a perceptually salient but probable event. A further experiment by Teglas and colleagues showed that if the occlusion time is prolonged enough, infants' reactions depend only on the numerosity of each object class. In this case, the occlusion duration was long (i.e., 2 seconds), so that infants could imagine that the objects continued to bounce inside the container, moving near and far from the opening. The results showed that infants looked reliably longer at the exit of the singleton than at the exit of one of the identical objects, regardless of their pre-occlusion distance from the opening. Indeed, the singleton exit was the less likely outcome given any sort of pre-occlusion configuration.

In sum, before acquiring language, infants appear to possess a surprisingly sophisticated ability to form rational expectations about future events: At 12 months, they are able to consider the respective possibilities of the various outcomes in a dynamical scene, by integrating numerical, spatial and temporal cues in a coherent way.

Conclusions

Taken together, the studies discussed in this chapter strongly support the hypothesis that naïve individuals can draw correct probabilistic inferences by applying extensional procedures (Johnson-Laird et al., 1999). The reviewed studies have documented that from early in their development individuals have an intuition of chance based on an extensional treatment of possibilities. In particular, these studies showed that: 1) preschool children are able to correctly assess prior (Brainerd, 1981; Davis, 1965; Goldberg, 1966; Yost et al., 1962) as well as posterior probability (Girotto and Gonzalez, 2008); 2) school children are able to predict the occurrence of a relation on the basis of its probability (Gonzalez and Girotto, 2011); 3) even preverbal or barely verbal infants possess elementary probabilistic intuitions (Teglas et al., 2007, 2011).

An extensional treatment of possibilities does not always yield correct inferences. Consider, for example, the following problem (adapted from Gonzalez and Girotto, 2011):

> This bag contains three black chips and one white chip. I'll shake the bag, and you'll take two chips from it at the same time, without looking. Do you think you will take two chips of two different colours or two chips of the same colour?

Most respondents, both children and adults, predict to take two chips of the same colour (Girotto and Gonzalez, 2011/Experiment 1). This answer is incorrect. Indeed, the chances of taking two chips of the same colour are the same as those of taking two chips of two different colours. Such a biased evaluation may depend on the tendency to focus on the chips of the predominant colour. If you focus on one of the black chips, you might notice that for each of them there are two twin-chips and only one chip of a different colour. Thus, you might be tempted to conclude that it is more likely to take two chips of the same colour. Tendencies of this sort indicate that in some cases naïve individuals fail to consider all possibilities necessary for a proper extensional treatment. The existence of these limits, however, does not undermine the view that naïve probabilistic reasoning is grounded on basic extensional intuitions. More importantly, these limits do not offer any support for the alternative, pessimistic accounts of naïve reasoning. In fact, the picture of probabilistic cognition that emerges from the results discussed in this chapter contradicts all these accounts.

Contrary to the Piagetian view that young children do not possess any probabilistic intuitions (Piaget and Inhelder, 1951/1975), the reviewed studies showed that preschoolers and even infants form rational expectations about uncertain events. Contrary to the hypothesis that the human mind can reason probabilistically only about sequences of events experienced in the past (Cosmides and Tooby, 1996; Gigerenzer and Hoffrage, 1995), the reviewed studies showed that preschoolers and even infants have correct probabilistic intuitions about single events never experienced in the past. Finally, contrary to the claim that the ability to make correct predictions about combinations of properties depends on formal instruction (Fischbein, 1975), the reviewed studies showed that children exhibit this ability before receiving any formal training in probability and combinatorics.

The question of the role of instruction in shaping naïve probabilistic reasoning leads us to consider the future directions of the reviewed work. Many authors have defended the thesis that probabilistic reasoning is not intuitive, and that only the acquisition of the probability calculus allows individuals to reason correctly about uncertain events (e.g., Nisbett, Kranz, Jepson and Kunda, 1983; Piattelli-Palmarini, 1994). Some authors have defended this thesis on the basis of an historical argument, namely, the recent invention of the probabilistic calculus: "Probabilities and percentages took millennia of literacy and numeracy to evolve; organisms did not acquire information in terms of probabilities and percentages until very recently" (Gigerenzer and Hoffrage, 1995, p. 686).

One main problem with this argument is that it neglects the evidence that, well before the emergence of the probability calculus in the seventeenth century, individuals living in pre-modern times had some notion of logical as well as aleatory probability (Franklin, 2001). In particular, there are written traces that medieval authors correctly conceptualized chance devices like the throwing of dice (e.g., Girotto and Gonzalez, 2005). For example, Dante (*Purgatory*, Canto VI, 1-4) referred to a game that consisted in guessing the outcome of a throw of two or three dice. In the fourteenth century, his commentators described the game by relying on the principle that the expectation of a given outcome depends on the number of ways in which it can be obtained: "The die is a cube which can land on each of its faces, so that the number made up in more ways must occur more often" della Lana, 1324–28/ 1866–67). "Reasonably, the sum that can be made up in more ways must occur more often than those that can be made up in one or two ways" (da Buti, 1385–95/1852–62). In sum, individuals living before the advent the probability calculus correctly evaluated chance by means of the same extensional principles as those of the present day naïve individuals.

These pieces of evidence vindicate Locke's (1690/1975) view that individuals were able to reason correctly even before the emergence of the formal systems of reasoning. His Aristotelian opponents claimed that only the acquisition of the Aristotelian syllogistic system allowed individuals to draw valid inferences. Their claim anticipated the present day psychologists' thesis that only the acquisition of the probability calculus allows individuals to reason probabilistically. Against such a claim, Locke argued:

> He that will look into many parts of Asia and America, will find men reason there perhaps as acutely as himself, who yet never heard of a syllogism, nor can reduce any one argument to those forms [. . .] Syllogism [is] not the great instrument of reason [. . .] if syllogisms must be taken for the only proper instrument and means of knowledge; it will follow, that before Aristotle there was no man that did or could know anything by reason; and that since the invention of syllogisms there is not one of ten thousand that doth. But God has not been so sparing to Men to make them barely two-legged creatures, and left to Aristotle to make them rational.
>
> (Locke, 1690/1975, p. 671)

The reviewed evidence concerning the probabilistic intuitions of children and pre-modern time individuals proves that Locke's view was correct. Just as Aristotle did not make humans rational by creating a normative system of deductive inferences, Pascal and Fermat did not make them rational by creating a normative system of probabilistic inferences. There is, however, a missing piece of evidence in this defence of Locke's view, namely, looking "into many parts of Asia and America" to prove that correct probabilistic intuitions exist in all human cultures. So far, no empirical study has addressed the issue of whether illiterate individuals who live in traditional societies are able to reason correctly about probabilities. Based on the reviewed work, we predict that these individuals will be able to do so by using the same extensional procedures discovered in investigating children's and untutored individuals' reasoning. More generally, the reviewed work leads us to make the bold claim that all human beings possess a correct, albeit elementary, intuition of probability, regardless of their education and cultural background. If proved correct, this claim would favor the view that basic probabilistic cognition, like basic arithmetic (e.g., Pica et al., 2004), is a universal component of the human mind.

Acknowledgements

Preparation of this article was supported by grants from the Italian Ministry of Universities (PRIN- 2010RP5NM) and from SwissandGlobal and Fondazione Ca' Foscari. The author is grateful to Wim De Neys and Magda Osman for their comments, and all the colleagues, in particular Michel Gonzalez, who made the studies reviewed in this article possible.

References

Barth, H., Le Mont, K., Lipton, J. and Spelke, E. S. (2005). Abstract number and arithmetic in preschool children. *Proceedings of the National Academy of Science, 102*, 14116–14121.

Beck, S. R. and Robinson, E. J. (2001). Children's ability to make tentative interpretations of ambiguous messages. *Journal of Experimental Child Psychology*, *79*, 95–114.

Brainerd, C. J. (1981). Working memory and the developmental analysis of probability judgment. *Psychological Review*, *88*, 463–502.

Cosmides, L. and Tooby, J. (1996). Are humans good intuitive statisticians after all? Rethinking some conclusions from the literature on judgment under uncertainty. *Cognition*, *58*, 1–73.

da Buti, F. (1852–1862). *Commento di Francesco da Buti sopra La Divina Commedia di Dante Allighieri*, [Francesco da Buti's commentary of Dante's Comedy]. Pisa: Nistri. (Orig. written circa 1385). Available at http://dante.dartmouth.edu/commentaries.php

Davies, H. (1965). Development of the probability concept in children. *Child Development*, *36*, 779–788.

della Lana, J. (1866–1867). *Comedia di Dante degli Allagherii col commento di Jacopo della Lana bolognese*, [Dante's Comedy, commented by Jacopo della Lana from Bologna]. Bologna: Tipografia Regia (Orig. written circa 1324). Available at http://dante.dartmouth.edu/commentaries.php

Denison, S. and Xu, F. (2010). Twelve- to fourteen-month-old infants can predict single-event probability with large set sizes. *Developmental Science*, *13*, 798–803.

Fischbein, E. (1975). *The intuitive sources of probabilistic thinking in children*. Dordrecht: Reidel.

Fischbein, E. and Schnarch, D. (1997). The evolution with age of probabilistic, intuitively based misconceptions. *Journal for Research in Mathematics Education*, *28*, 96–105.

Franklin, J. (2001). *The science of conjecture. Evidence and probability before Pascal*. Baltimore: John Hopkins University Press.

Gigerenzer, G. and Hoffrage, U. (1995) How to improve Bayesian reasoning without instruction: Frequency format. *Psychological Review*, *102*, 684–704.

Girotto, V. and Gonzalez, M. (2001). Solving probabilistic and statistical problems: A matter of information structure and question form. *Cognition*, *78*, 247–276.

Girotto, V. and Gonzalez, M. (2002). Chances and frequencies in probabilistic reasoning: Rejoinder to Hoffrage, Gigerenzer, Krauss, and Martignon. *Cognition*, *84*, 353–359.

Girotto, V. and Gonzalez, M. (2005). Probabilistic reasoning and combinatorial analysis. In V. Girotto and P. N. Johnson-Laird (Eds.) *The shape of reason*. New York: Psychology Press.

Girotto, V. and Gonzalez, M. (2008). Children's understanding of posterior probability. *Cognition*, *106*, 325–344.

Gonzalez, M. and Girotto, V. (2011). Combinatorics and probability. Six-to ten-year-olds reliably predict whether a relation will occur. *Cognition*, *20*, 372–379.

Goldberg, S. (1966). Probability judgments by preschool children: Task conditions and performance. *Child Development*, *37*, 157–167.

Hoffrage, U., Gigerenzer, G., Krauss, S. and Martignon, L. (2002). Representation facilitates reasoning: What natural frequencies are and what they are not. *Cognition*, *84* (3), 343–352.

Inhelder, B. and Piaget, J. (1964). *The early growth of logic*. London: Routledge and Kegan Paul. (Original work published 1955).

Johnson-Laird, P. N. (2006). *How we reason*. Oxford: Oxford University Press.

Johnson-Laird, P. N., Legrenzi, P., Girotto, V., Sonino-Legrenzi, M. and Caverni, J. P. (1999). Naïve probability: A model theory of extensional reasoning. *Psychological Review*, *106*, 62–88.

Kahneman, D., Slovic, P. and Tversky, A. (Eds.). (1982). *Judgment under uncertainty: Heuristics and biases*. Cambridge: Cambridge University Press.

Locke, J. (1975). *An essay concerning human understanding.* Oxford: Claredon Press. (Original work published 1690).

Nisbett, R. E., Krantz, D.H., Jepson, C. and Kunda, D. (1983). The use of statistical heuristics in everyday inductive reasoning. *Psychological Review, 90*, 339–363.

Piaget, J. (1950). Une expérience sur la psychologie du hasard chez l'enfant: Le tirage au sort des couples. *Acta Psychologica, 7*, 323–336.

Piaget, J. and Inhelder, B. (1975). *The origin of the idea of chance in children.* New York: Norton. (Original work published 1951).

Piaget, J. and Szeminska, B. (1952). *The child's conception of number*. New York: Humanities Press. (Original work published 1941).

Piatelli-Palmarini, M. (1994). *Inevitable illusions: How mistakes of reason rule our minds.* New York: Wiley.

Pica, P., Lerner, C., Izard, V. and Dehaene, S. (2004). Exact and approximate arithmetic in an Amazonian indigene group. *Science, 306*, 499–503.

Spelke, E. S. (1990). Principles of object perception. *Cognitive Science, 14*, 29–56.

Surian, L., Caldi, S. and Sperber, D. (2007). Attribution of beliefs by 13-month-old infants. *Psychological Science, 18*, 580–586.

Teglas, E., Girotto, V., Gonzalez, M. and Bonatti, L.L. (2007). Intuitions of probabilities shape expectations about the future at 12 months and beyond. *Proceedings of the National Academy of Science, 104*, 19156–19159.

Teglas, E., Vul, E., Girotto, V., Gonzalez, M., Tennembaum, J.B. and Bonatti, L.L. (2011). Pure reasoning in 12-month-old infants as probabilistic inference. *Science*, 332, 1054–1059.

Tversky, A. and Kahneman, D. (1983). Extensional versus intuitive reasoning: The conjunction fallacy in probability judgment. *Psychological Review, 90*, 293–315.

Yost, P. A., Siegel, A. E. and Andrews, J. M. (1962). Nonverbal probability judgments by young children. *Child Development, 33*, 769–780.

Wynn, K. (1992) Addition and subtraction by human infants. *Nature*, 358, 749–750.

8 Reasoning research

Where was it going? Where is it now? Where will it be going?

Magda Osman

Introduction

The aim of this book is to mark the trends in reasoning research and to give the reader a sense of the potential directions, themes, techniques, issues and questions that reflect modern psychological investigations on reasoning behaviour. Before doing the obligatory round up of what we can learn from work to date, the first part of this discussion will consider the historical origins of reasoning research and the major issues and research themes that have emerged. This tackles the first question of the title: *Where was reasoning research going?* From this, the second part of the discussion considers the research ideas presented in this book and draws together the common themes that connect the various different research strands. This then tackles the second question: *Where is reasoning research now?* This also helps to set up the discussion up for the final section, the aim of which is to make some predictions about where research on reasoning is heading. There must be room for speculation on occasion, and in the role of editor and author, I have been given a great privilege to use this book as a forum to do just that, so this section is where I will discuss what I think. This then is my own reflection in response to the final question: *Where is reasoning researching going?*

Where was reasoning research going?

The early days of reasoning research: finding its way

If we look back to psychological research on reasoning such as the work of Wason (1960, 1961,1966, 1968, 1969), and Henle (1962) in the 60s, and even earlier work by Deutsch (1956) and Woodworth and Sells (1935), we see a field emerging from the midst of logic. Logical reasoning was heralded as the hallmark of adulthood from work by Piaget (1952), and was the defining approach of scientists thanks to Popper's (1952) hypo-deductive method. The dominating position then was that we aspire to logic, and if we are a well-rounded fully developed adult with all our faculties intact, then we should think analytically and come to logical conclusions as a result. What this also means is that we evaluate arguments, carefully think through evidence and are mindful and cautious that our initial intuitions and beliefs may not be the ones we should act on. Are we capable of thinking in this way? To answer this, in the 60s, 70s Wason (and collaborators, Jonathan Evans, Philip Johnson-Laird, Diane Shapiro) gave reasoning researchers three tools that launched the basis for examining the structure of thought, and the process by which we make inferences: the Wason (1966) selection task (conditional reasoning task); Wason's (1960) 2-4-6 task (hypothesis testing problem); and Wason and Brooks' (1979) THOG task (disjunctive reasoning task). His work took psychologists down an uncomfortable direction. It made them get to grips with evidence showing that people's reasoning deviates systematically from the uniquely human and rational mode of thought we are supposed to have, namely logic. In fact it brought into question whether there are ever situations in which the structure of our thoughts aligns with that of logic. Perhaps we simply aren't built to think in a logical way. But if we don't have logic to judge when we are thinking correctly and when we aren't, what is the best bench mark for evaluating the rationality of our reasoning? Controversially, some researchers denied the very existence of reasoning errors (e.g., Henle, 1962). Others agreed that reasoning performance was flawed, and standard logic could not account for naïve individuals' inferences. But they refused the traditional view (e.g., Piaget) that standard logic is a good yard stick for human reasoning competence. Instead, they argued that a 'natural' logic could appropriately capture the actual reasoning process that researchers were uncovering (e.g., Braine, 1978; Ennis, 1976; Johnson-Laird, 1975; Osherson, 1975). Though many disagreements would ensue about precisely what 'natural' logic should look like.

Generally the findings from the mainstream reasoning research at the time suggested to the academic world and beyond that, at best, humans make inferences based on information that they can call to mind quickly. What people do is draw speedy conclusions which can rarely be defended on any rational basis. The conclusions that reasoners draw are strongly held. Their attachment to the conclusions they've drawn seems to suggest a certain inflexibility to appreciate alternative ways of construing the task. If this was the case, then why is it that people draw the same kinds of systematically erroneous conclusions? The obvious research step was to ask reasoners to give insights into their own thinking processes, and articulate the reasons for the conclusions that they would draw in reasoning tasks. This approach revealed that people could rarely sensibly defend the inferences they made, and that the match between a logical rationalization and their inferences was merely a lucky coincidence (Evans and Wason, 1976).

Of course Wason was not the only researcher to show that our reasoning ability wasn't quite as we hoped. Given the historical context in which research on reasoning was conducted, a fair amount of work was concerned with logical operations in children and adolescents (Lawson, 1978; Mogar, 1960; Roberge, 1970). Moreover, much of the work around the 50s right through to the mid-70s focused on the associations between deductive reasoning (typically syllogistic reasoning, transitive inference and conditional reasoning) and other cognitive processes (e.g., spatial processing, mathematical problem solving) (Cofer, 1957; Collis, 1971; Hunterlocher, 1968), as well as connections to general intelligence and verbal ability (Sternberg, 1977). Research at this time gave us confirmation bias in hypothesis testing and conditional reasoning (Wason and Johnson-Laird, 1972), and errors in syllogistic reasoning such as atmosphere, figural and conversion errors (Johnson-Laird and Steedman, 1978). These were the go-to examples of behaviours associated with deductive reasoning, and they could be reliably demonstrated through simple paper and pencil techniques. Around that time, efforts were also being made to examine the extent to which speed of generating a response was associated with performance in reasoning tasks (Kagan, Pearson and Welch, 1966; Marcus and Rips, 1979; Valett, 1966). In some cases there was little association (Kintsch and Monk, 1972). A rather sour picture is emerging, that no matter how long people spend reasoning deductively they are still going to be hopelessly bad.

Without question, the major message that came out of work in the 60s and 70s was that human reasoning is somewhat flawed. The only major concessional point being that, while we are biased, our biased reasoning probably comes in useful in some situations in the real world, and perhaps there is a duality in the way our reasoning system is constructed. But, we'd fallen very far from the graces of logic and probability theory that were once argued to be the foundations of adult thought and reasoned action. Researchers were telling us that we were mostly reasoning by intuition, worse still, we were fundamentally irrational.

The establishment of the psychology of reasoning: coming into its own

The aftertaste from work up until the late 70s was marginally unpleasant. Partly as an overhang of the findings from Wason's tools for studying reasoning, several uncomfortable issues were being raised and would dog reasoning research across the next two decades. *Are we irrational? Perhaps deductive reasoning tools aren't the best way of examining human reasoning? If that's the case, what should we be using to study human reasoning? Perhaps our normative model is wrong? What is the right normative model to apply to human reasoning? Perhaps the explanations for these deviations lie in the origins of man, and the contexts in which particular kinds of reasoning were needed that logic tasks don't capture?*

First things first, is it the measurement tools that are the problem, or is it us? A key theoretical idea that carried over from the 70s into the 80s, and in fact continues to make a substantial contribution to date – as evidenced in the work discussed in this book – is that reasoning is made up of two fundamentally different processes. This idea would help salvage the position that humans have the capability of logical thought, but that we also deviate from this systematically because we have an intuitive system of thinking. Since the work by Wason and Evans (1975), dual-process theories set out the view that we have two ways of reasoning, one of which is analytic and the other which is intuitive. What prompted this type of processing distinction was the fact that what people said about how they reason, and what people did in terms of their actual observable inferences were contradictory. This finding implicated a key milestone in research in cognitive psychology in the 80s.

At the time Ericsson and Simon's (1980, 1985) work on self-reports, suggested that, broadly speaking, the verbal descriptions that people gave about the reasons behind their behaviour are influenced by what information can be called to memory. If details can't be drawn from memory then people often give rationalizations, that is, they infer the basis of their behaviour, rather than knowing why they did what they did. But, in general, the matter of concern for Ericsson and Simon was that evidence of inconsistencies between what is verbally reported and other measures of behaviour is largely down to poor experimental procedures psychologists used. The clearer and cleaner and more systematic the measure of verbal and non-verbal behaviour the more likely the apparent dissociation between conscious and non-conscious disappears. Actually, in the midst of Ericsson and Simon's work, an opposing position on the validity of verbal reports was being made by Nisbett and Wilson (1977). The evidence from the world of reasoning research was consistent with their position, which was that across various domains of cognitive psychology and social psychology introspective reports were largely inaccurate and based predominately on post-hoc rationalizations. In the main, Nisbett and Wilson were suggesting that participants in psychology experiments may not have accurate insight into the processes that support their behaviour, and this is why they can't give verbal accurate descriptions of the reasons behind their behaviour. In the realm of reasoning, the view was that the processes people were actually using to solve deductive reasoning problems were not the same as the descriptions people were giving of their reasoning processes (Evans and Wason, 1975; Wason and Evans, 1975). The explanation for this finding was that the rationalizations that people gave suggested that they had little real idea why they reasoned the way they did. This was because the underlying reason for their solutions was based on intuition and the operations of intuition were not accessible to consciousness. This indeed was the speculation by researchers at the time (Evans, 1984). It became de rigueur to show that people did not possess accurate self-insight into the processes that lead to their inferences and conclusions (Evans, Ball and Brooks, 1987). A happy consequence of this research line is that it took the pressure of arguing against the validity of researchers' go to tools of measurement (e.g., Wason selection task, syllogisms). From this point of view we could argue that it's not the tools, it's us that is the problem. It's just that while we have the capacity to reason logically, a lot of the time we reason intuitively, and sometimes our intuitions takes us in the wrong direction; that's what standard reasoning tasks are able to show. From this standpoint reasoning researchers could breathe a sigh of relief, there wasn't any need to abandon the tools.

However, the issue as to whether reasoning researchers were using the right tools for the job was being called into question in a different area, developmental reasoning. While the theoretical views of Piaget influenced researchers on adult reasoning in the 60s and 70s, a more dedicated approach to studying children and adolescent's reasoning skills was gaining momentum in the 80s. The resounding message here was that failures to help train children and adults into logical thinking, by teaching them logic, also supported those theorists calling into question whether reasoning tools were valid assessments of thinking (Cheng, Holyoak, Nisbett and Oliver, 1986; O'Brien and Overton, 1982).

Perhaps as a result of the issues concerning the validity of deductive reasoning tasks, or because there was more exploration into varied phenomena associated with reasoning, or perhaps because popularity in reasoning research was growing anyway in the 80s, the breadth of reasoning phenomena being studied was expanding. Research efforts were being focused on scientific reasoning (Dunbar and Klahr, 1989); statistical reasoning (Nisbett, Krantz, Jepson and Kunda, 1983); evaluations of methods for examining probabilistic reasoning (Cohen, 1981); analogical reasoning (Gentner, 1989; Vosniadou and Ortony, 1989); causal reasoning (Trabasso, Secco and Broek, 1984); verbal reasoning (Read, 1981) and moral reasoning (Haan, Weiss and Johnson, 1982). Moreover, studies were including additional psychological measures of reasoning behaviour such as reaction times (Cherniak, 1984; Leahey, 1980). Comparisons were being made between abstract logical rules and certain types of contextualized versions of reasoning tasks which involved social rules and regulations (Cheng and Holyoak, 1985; Galotti, 1989; Griggs and Cox, 1982). Actually, some work in the mid-70s did focus on what was termed 'abstract versus realistic reasoning' (Wason and Shapiro, 1971), and showed some improvement when a realistic context was used. The upshot from the work in the 80s was that the reason why our intuition is so useful in the real world is that it is tuned to making inferences about rules and regulations that matter, i.e. social ones.

Given the broadening of the research horizons around the 80s, by the time we move into the late 90s, reasoning research has shifted dramatically away from focusing on uncovering the limits of deductive reasoning, but instead exploring the links with other cognitive faculties (verbal fluency, language, reading, working memory, attention). In fact there is an explosion of interest in reasoning research in general in the 90s. While people are still debating if our representational reasoning system is rule-based (Rips, 1999) or mental model-based (Johnson-Laird, 1999), we also have a parallel debate concerning whether our representational system is associative-based or rule-based (Sloman, 1996; Sloman and Rips, 1998). Neuropsychological issues are becoming fashionable and techniques from this field are finding their way into reasoning research (Goel, Gold, Kapur and Houle, 1997; Wharton and Grafman, 1998). It is also at this stage that inspection-time techniques are introduced as a method of uncovering the involvement of the unconscious in reasoning through attentional processes (Evans, 1996). The inspection-time paradigm was based on a mouse-tracking methodology to measure card inspection times, which was later developed by Ball, Lucas, Miles and Gale (2003) into an eye-tracking version. The role of culture and evolution is taking centre stage notably spearheaded by Cosmides and Tooby (1994) and Gigerenzer and Hug (1992). In parallel, building on their earlier work, Holyoak and Cheng's (1995) claims about the role of social rules was taking off. They were suggesting that social pragmatic factors are key to the way we reason, and this is why the context in which reasoning tasks are situated can be so successful in facilitating reasoning performance. In any case, be it culture, evolution, or social pragmatic rules, the argument made in these circles is that there is very little to learn from abstract deductive reasoning tasks, instead the key to understanding the mechanisms and functions of reasoning is through context. Interest in spatial, analogical, inductive, scientific and causal reasoning is reaching a point where there is specific research communities dedicated to each one of these areas. The dominating frameworks of the day are Johnson-Laird's (1999) mental models; Rips' (1999) mental rules; Oaksford and Chater's (1994; 1999) Bayesian inference models; and Sperber's relevance theory (Sperber, Cara and Girotto, 1995). In addition, three topics are pervading most research studies on reasoning in one shape or form, and they are rationality, probabilistic reasoning and dual-reasoning processes.

Recent years in reasoning research: facing a midlife crisis or time for a change?

If we compare the directions of research in the 80s and 90s with the directions taken in the last decade, the field of reasoning is clearly fractured. Certain issues are on the wane. For instance, the debate concerning whether our representational system is mental rule-based or mental model-based appears to have become somewhat of a niche concern. Understanding the limits of deductive reasoning has also become a niche issue, in fact outside of belief-bias effects in syllogistic reasoning, it seems that few researchers focus on conversion errors, atmosphere errors and figural errors. In essence the psychology of reasoning can't be identified as simply the ability to reasoning logically or not, not any more. But perhaps this is a good thing since at best this would be a bad caricature of our reasoning process. Reasoning research has tended to have a fraught relationship with logic, once the realisation came about that humans don't think according to certain types of logic, researchers became critical of logic as a useful benchmark. Perhaps because now the position logic has in reasoning is not quite as strong, we can now listen to what logicians have to say about logic. Philosophers and logicians have long since known that there are many types of syntax, semantics and parameters that can be specified in logic which means there are many ways of capturing the appropriate mode of human reasoning given certain conditions. The fact that psychologists have only focused on a certain type of classical logic to judge human reasoning against reflects a misunderstanding of the nuances of logic (Stenning and van Lambalgen, 2008). As reasoning researchers, many of us have come to believe that when it comes to logic, form not content matters. The dry application of rules regardless of the nuances of the context should be the pinnacle of reasoning. Spanning the 60 or so years of research on the psychology of reasoning, we know that humans just don't do that. Humans simply don't dryly go about applying the same set of logical rules consistently regardless of what context we are in. But, logicians have been saying that reasoning researchers shouldn't be doing that either. Context matters in the real world, and in logic, context can also matter.

Reasoning in one shape or form is a process that transforms information to generate new information. We have shifted away from using logic to understand this process, and for some time now we look to understanding the inference process, but examining how we use probabilities and beliefs to guide the conclusions we draw. The popular research interests now are a mix of old and new. If we take the themes that emerge in the last major conferences and workshops (e.g., Cognitive

Science Society Meeting 2012, 2011, 2010; International Conference on Thinking 2012), as well as the published work on the Web of Science 2000–2013, reasoning research tends to focus on five key interests: 1) the link between reasoning ability and memory; 2) moral reasoning; 3) causal reasoning; 4) probabilistic reasoning – and associates such as inductive reasoning (or some might argue are one in the same); and 5) dual-process reasoning.

Not all of these themes are represented in the present book in fact the key theme of the chapters here is centred round point five. In the main this is because the issue of dual-processes has a long history and is hugely pervasive as a theoretical position that implicates moral (Haidt, 2001), probabilistic (De Neys, Vartanian and Goel, 2008) and causal reasoning (Fugelsang and Thompson, 2003). Moreover, it concerns the role between reasoning and memory, since the different underlying reasoning systems are thought to have different relationships as to how they draw on memory, and the demands they make on memory processes (De Neys, 2006). Also, as a result of researcher's interests in uncovering the precise differences and relationships between the two speculated mechanisms, evolutionary theories are still relatively popular and have helped to draw in a community of comparative psychologists. Why? Because one of the systems we have is thought to be an evolutionary old mechanism and involves basic associative mechanisms. Which is why researchers are asking: *Do we have a basic associative mechanism that allows us to reason, much like animals?* This takes the approach that humans have a basic computational process that enables some form of reasoning to take place that animals (e.g., rats, pigeons, chimps) also possess. The ever expanding interest in causal reasoning also adds to this debate (Blaisdell, Sawa, Leising and Waldman, 2006). Researchers are asking if the explicit cause-effect relations not only form the basis of most of human reasoning, but that animals also demonstrate some basic causal reasoning as well (e.g., bees, rats, chimps). This is a rehashing of the rule-associations debate, but transported into the forum of animal research, and with a causal spin. The positive upshot of this is that it is taking reasoning researchers into a different community, one which never had much concern with it before. With some exceptions (e.g., McGonigle and Chalmers, 1977, 1992), this was mostly popular in the early days of concept learning in the 50s and 60s in which animal and human research was focused on concept and category formation, and whether it developed through associations or rules (Bruner, Goodnow and Austin, 1956; Hunt, 1962; Levine, 1966).

The current status quo of reasoning research

One of the objectives of this book was that it would introduce the reader to new research techniques and themes that are building momentum in reasoning research. One question worth considering is, what are these new empirical techniques and research directions designed to investigate? In the main, as suggested earlier, in my view, the overarching focus of these research themes is the dual-process approach to conceptualising human reasoning. Let's now consider what these various methods and technologies are.

Do we reason a certain way because of our genes?

With new technologies – and revisiting established ones – we are beginning to investigate a whole range of phenomena that were never open to reasoning research. For instance, the role of biology in mental function was the focus of Stollstoff's chapter. In the last 10 years there has been a trend to bring together molecular genetics, neuroscience and psychology as a way to understand how genes influence the mind by shaping the brain. This new field of research termed 'Cognitive Neurogenetics' has helped uncover the relationship between genetic variation and brain function. As controversial as this sounds, the work by Stollstoff suggests just that the way we reason is influenced by our genes. For a start, she argues that the process of reasoning is not independent of emotions. Stollstoff shows that the fact that there is a link between emotion and reasoning is because of our genes. Interestingly, individual differences here refers to the way in which people differ according to whether they have more long or short alleles (the position of DNA coding on a chromosome), and this is why some people succumb to the bias more than others. Stollstoff shows that the release of serotonin, a neurotransmitter typically associated with emotions such as anxiety, is based on the functioning of the transporter protein which is designed to regulate the use and uptake of serotonin. The genotype that is associated with the transporter protein is 5-HTTLPR. There is variation in the genotype 5-HTTLPR, which in turn leads to variation in brain function. Interestingly the variation in brain function can be identified by reasoning tasks such as syllogisms either with emotionally laden content, or neutral versions, both of which were designed by Stollstoff and colleagues to include belief-bias inducing versions, and non-belief-bias inducing versions. The headline result is that if we are susceptible to emotional reactivity – which is an intense reaction to externally inducing emotional stimuli – then we're more likely to fall foul of the belief-bias effect.

This research stream shows that, at least according to the conventions set down early in the history of research in psychology, our error-prone reasoning is the result of interference from our beliefs and our emotions. Moreover, people who are more susceptible to the emotional content of the reasoning tasks, and in turn more susceptible to the belief bias, find it harder to inhibit their emotional processing. Similarly, the same inhibitory mechanism associated with the right inferior prefrontal cortex (rIPC) thought to be involved in blocking the processing of beliefs, has also been implicated in the blocking of negative emotional content in belief-bias tasks. The activity in this region is associated with the extent to which the belief bias is found. In other words, if you're genetically disposed to emotional reactivity, you are more likely to show reduced activity in one brain region (rIPC) and increased activity in the another brain region (ventral medial prefrontal cortex [vmPFC]), which means it is less likely to inhibit your processing of emotional stimuli, which in turn will lead to more biases in reasoning on belief-bias tasks. Neuroscience and neurogenetics are not concerned with whether or not we are rational or logical, but rather, the extent to which emotions and beliefs play a role in the way we reason. The bottom line of this research is that the degree of control we have over our beliefs and emotions in order to make inferences is down to neurological mechanisms and genetic differences. Interestingly, this bypasses a lot of work that explains the involvement of beliefs and emotions in reasoning at the behavioural level. The other key theme that unites the work from neuroscience and neurogenetics is the inhibitory mechanism we use to prevent the interference of beliefs and emotions while trying to reason analytically. Clearly the implication is that that we have a type of meta-cognitive process, or a process of cognitive control that is activated from time to time. The functional basis for a meta-cognitive process is also considered in Trémolière and Bonnefon's chapter. While Stollstoff's work shows at a neuroscientific and neurogentic level that emotions can interfere with rational thoughts, Trémolière and Bonnefon's work shows that negative thoughts, such as thoughts of death can be extremely detrimental to reasoning rationally.

Do thoughts of death interfere with rational thinking?

The work discussed by Trémolière and Bonnefon suggests that actually there should be special attention directed towards the saliency of thoughts of death, and their debilitating impact on analytical forms of reasoning. The main manipulation simply involves asking people to write down their emotions when thinking about their own death, and describe the details of the physical process of their own death. The many demonstrations that are discussed by Trémolière and Bonnefon, ranging from belief bias in syllogistic reasoning tasks, moral reasoning problems and probabilistic reasoning tasks, all show that thoughts of death significantly impact on the ability to make a normatively accurate response. The general claim being made is that, consistent with Stollstoff, we have a mechanism or process of reasoning that is based on representations from semantic memory, or emotional content, and there is a mechanism or process that tries to surmount these representations in order to think through and reason from a problem by focusing on the logical relations in the problem. A mechanism of some kind is needed to prevent the inference of beliefs and emotions, or as in the case of Trémolière and Bonnefon, its thoughts of death. Behavioural work in the study of reasoning tells us also that trying to inhibit intuitive beliefs takes up a lot of processing effort and time. Remarkably, the work by Trémolière and Bonnefon suggest that inhibiting thoughts of death take up as much processing effort, or perhaps more processing effort than typical experimental interventions such as dual tasks.

The important question that this work raises that forms the discussion of Trémolière and Bonnefon's chapter is what function does the debilitating effect of thinking about death have on our reasoning faculties? As it is, they suggest that this effect may not be localized to reasoning, in which case, we may be significantly impaired in our usual cognitive activities whenever thoughts of death loom large. And so this question extends to the role of emotions and beliefs in reasoning. It might be the case that the saliency of death thoughts is stronger than other thoughts and emotionally anxious experiences, but overall, the work discussed across the two chapters shows that they impact on our analytical thinking. What function, then, do they serve? For Trémolière and Bonnefon, the answer is one of evolution. The speculation is that perhaps the cost of having a sophisticated meta-cognitive process means that we, unlike other animals, are aware of our own death. The functional advantage of this is that we pursue activities that increase our longevity. But the preoccupation of thoughts of death and reminders of the end in turn require a sophisticated mechanism to inhibit them. What we end up with is a battle between a need to think about our mortality as a motivator to survive, while at the same time avoiding the continual thoughts of death in order to carry out our daily tasks. Whether or not the mechanism behind coping with the thoughts of death is evolutionary one is worth further speculation. For instance, one would need to establish the modular component rather than the general mechanisms involved. In addition, the problem of implicating meta-cognitive processes into an evolutionary based explanation start getting researchers into the sticky ground of the Cartesian Theatre (Dennett and Kinsbourne, 1992). One speculation might be that it's not that we have a devoted evolved mechanism for attenuating negative thinking about death *per se*, but simply that this attenuating is a hedonic by-product (reduction of negative thoughts and feelings) of the discounting behaviours triggered by mortality salience cues (and there will be some individual variation in how effective those cues are). Nevertheless, the chapter brings to light a number of important issues, and what Trémolière and Bonnefon show is just how much of an impact thoughts of death can have on our reasoning process. If we take into account the message from the Stollstoff and Trémolière and Bonnefon chapters, both seem to show that there is some degree of difficulty in trying to reason free from the interferences of negative thoughts and emotions.

How do we block inferring thoughts when we try to reason?

The work by Borst, Moutier and Houdé has adapted the negative priming technique for the purposes of studying the inhibition of beliefs in reasoning tasks. The negative priming technique is typically used in studies of cognitive control, such as the Stroop task; though the effect isn't restricted to perceptual features, it generalizes to semantic features of stimuli as well. In essence the negative priming technique involves priming information that is not relevant in the current context, but relevant in a subsequent reasoning episode. The negative priming effect essentially shows that people (children and adults) spend a lot of time inhibiting the prime, that when it becomes useful later, rather than speed up responses – which is what primes usually do, it slows responses down. In other words, you've been told not to think about the elephant in the room, that when someone asks you where the elephant in the room is you're slower to give an answer. The work by Borst, Moutier, Houdé and collaborators has shown that the negative priming effect generalizes to tasks such as conditional reasoning, Piagetian mathematical reasoning tasks and syllogistic reasoning tasks. In their chapter, Borst, Moutier and Houdé explain that people struggle to respond quickly and accurately because there is a type of mental flip-flopping between representations that we needed to block, which is an effortful process, and switch to needing to unblock them, which in turn is an additional effortful process.

The key message from the Borst, Moutier and Houdé chapter is that this flip-flopping increases cognitive flexibility which is why, as with other executive control tasks, many have claimed that reasoning and thinking skills can be improved via practicing cognitive control. The implications here also mean that we might be better able to prevent the interference of beliefs and emotions, if we were better trained to exercise our cognitive control. Such training as this paves the way for further developmental and adult work in uncovering the links between reasoning and other cognitive faculties that require the same basic functional properties.

Can our eyes tell us something about how we reason?

The work by Ball and colleagues has shown that through eye-tracking techniques, the underlying biases that people have are reflected in what they attend to first and what they focus on when thinking and reasoning. Much of the work that is discussed throughout the different chapters of this book tends to suggest that at some level we have a default system or default representation, a default go-to set of beliefs, or a default emotional response. When we read through a reasoning problem, we have initially formulated a response based on ideas, beliefs, memories, emotions, that almost seem ready made, and they are also sticky. That is, they are hard to inhibit, or suppress; whichever flavor of override mechanism one is supporting. One of the questions that keeps recurring in the belief-bias literature, and also as a result of interest in dual-processes of reasoning, is whether we are prompted to do more analytical reasoning when something about the reasoning task doesn't add up, or whether the analytical reasoning is always going on but might have to work harder under some situations than others. This question is at the heart of Ball's work and it is through the techniques developed through eye-tracking measures that significant headway has been made.

To elaborate on the question, let's consider the first position. Our ideas, beliefs, memories, and emotions, may kick in when we see a believable argument, and so there isn't any need to evaluate it, we just accept it without much inspection. Whereas, our ideas, beliefs, memories and emotions will still kick in when we face a less believable argument, but this time, the doubt around whether to accept it or not, sends a signal to our analytic or evaluative reasoning process, which then means we spend more time thinking about the argument. That's one explanation, the other is that our analytic or evaluative reasoning process is always ticking by, but is for the most part going to give our ideas, beliefs, memories and emotions a helping hand, like a stamp of approval. It's only in rare cases when the analytic reasoning is going to override our initial ideas, beliefs, memories and emotions. Whichever explanation is preferred, both assume beliefs come first and then a form of evaluation/possible override comes in second. As mentioned already, this seems to be a view that underpins the work presented by Stollstoff, Trémolière and Bonnefon, and perhaps even Borst, Moutier and Houdé. The alternative to both these positions, is that when we are faced with arguments that invite us to think about them in context of knowledge we possess about the world, we start off evaluating the argument analytically. The degree of scrutiny depends on how uncertain we are about its believability (or plausibility). The more believable it is the less we scrutinize it. When we scrutinize it and we don't get anywhere and can't draw any conclusion, that's when we rely on our ideas, beliefs, memories, and emotions.

Ball's work actually tends to favor the latter position, which has significant implications beyond reasoning. Many popular science books (e.g., Thaler and Sunstein's (2008) *Nudge*, Kahneman's *Thinking, Fast and Slow* (2011), Gazzaniga's (2011) *Who's in Charge?*, to name but a few) are making claims that are pervading the public domain, and these are claims that are in line with a defaultist approach, which means our error prone initial ideas, beliefs, memories and emotions get in the way of our analytic thinking. The recommendation is that we need to spend time recognizing when to override these biased representations in order to think accurately, reasoning rationally, and make optimal decisions. The work by Ball and his lab suggest that our analytical thinking takes center stage most of the time, and that a breakdown or failure to resolve a problem, or find a solution, or draw a conclusion is the point at which our intuitive system comes to the rescue. Again, this issue brings us back to how we switch from one mode of reasoning to another, which in some shape or form is one of the recurring themes in this book, and a theme of interest in the general. For Ball, the work from the eye-tracking and inspection time approach is to suggest that perhaps internal judgments of confidence, uncertainty, or plausibility in the evaluation of the reasoning problem cue a switch between analytic to intuitive reasoning.

Can we make people believe they are analytic so that they can think that way?

The work by Augustinova and her lab blends well-known phenomena in the social psychology domain with typical behaviour reported in the psychology of reasoning research. The idea behind her research programme is to develop methods that build on social phenomena to identify the potential flexibility in our thinking. After all, if we can be made to induce a concept of ourselves that is confident and methodical and evaluative, then can we organize our cognitive processes in such a way as to implement an analytic mode of thinking that we would have been less likely to use before the intervention? The technique that Augustinova has developed, which has been demonstrated in reasoning, decision-making and problem solving, involves presenting participants with descriptions that create a strong association of desirable attributes of a particular style of thinking. In this case the style of thinking is rational, and the attributes associated with it are academic success, successful professional careers and job satisfaction. There was further stage of evaluation and identification with this desirable mode of thinking, which led to a sort of social task set – task set being an experimental procedure for inducing a particular pattern of responding, in this case, responding rationally. Remarkably the findings suggest that when people are encouraged to think and identify with a particular style of thinking, it can be used to successfully induce actual reasoning which could be classified as rational. The early work by Wason developed "cognitive therapies" that were designed to encourage people to think logically through various indirect approaches. Some of the methods involved asking participants to go through a process of evaluation in which considered the implications for a rule if different options were explored. Or else, the therapies involved changing the context of the problem from an abstract one to a thematic or realistic real world context (Wason and Shapiro, 1971). This latter method was made popular by Griggs and Cox (1982), and Manketelow and Evans (1979). They showed that in effect, people could be "primed" to think about logical relations in everyday contexts in which violations occurred. The problem for many researchers was that the way in which people evaluated everyday contexts failed to generalize beyond the everyday deontic contexts that induced correct reasoning in the first place. The work by Augustinova takes this one step further. By priming a mode of thinking, Augustinova shows that, in effect, rational thinking can be applied to which ever context the reasoner is faced with. It's as if inducing people to believe they are thinking rationally fine tunes their reasoning faculties in that direction.

One issue that Augustinova addresses, which has important implications for this kind of work, is to what extent are people convinced by the active self-concept they are induced to have? The claims made by Augustinova are that people adopt their new self-concept willingly, depending on how socially desirable it is. The way people do this is that they begin to recruit examples from memory that support or even embellish the self-concept they are currently identifying with. This argument points to two things. For a start it tells us that our meta-cognitive processes are good at maintaining coherence. We have a general self-concept and our working self-concept, both of which are made to cohere, otherwise we'd constantly doubt who we are. The second important point takes us down two paths. Either we clearly are more competent in reasoning correctly (according to the convention that the reasoning researcher has laid down) than we would perhaps recognize, and changing the self-concept is a way of uncovering this. Or, we need a helping hand to match our self-belief (which is that we are generally rational/logical) with a set of associates which reinforce a competency that we have, but don't always use. The jury may be out as to which of the two interpretations best suits the data, but nevertheless, it is encouraging that there is evidence to show that we have a way of thinking analytically that generalizes to multiple contexts.

Do we all fundamentally possess the ability to reason correctly?

The developmental work by Girotto and his colleagues suggests that, when it comes to reasoning about uncertainty, we do indeed possess the basic probabilistic intuitions that enable us to reason correctly. This capability was shown with babies as young as 12-months old. The kinds of techniques Girotto and his lab have developed focus on measuring infants' looking time to events with different probabilities, not unlike the work of Ball and his collaborators. The basic idea being that the longer children spend looking at particular stimuli as compared with control stimuli, researchers can infer the amount of value or saliency attached to those stimuli. In the case of children and babies, the extended looking time implies surprise; by looking away they are indicating that the outcome was one that was expected. This paradigm is based on a principle that developmental researcher follow which is that infants tend to look loner to unexpected events, namely events that violate their expectations. Indeed, studies using looking time techniques suggest that infants have expectations about arithmetic facts (e.g., Wynn, 1992), physics principles (e.g., Spelke, 1994) and social interactions (e.g., Hamlin, Wynn and Bloom, 2007).

Simple animations that have been used are built on the principle of probability, albeit a simple one. For instance, a box containing a number of similar objects and one very different object was the basis for many of the studies reported by Girotto, and the key manipulations focused on the object that escaped the box. In some cases it was the more probable one, and in other cases it was the rare one. Interestingly babies would look more on occasions when the rare object escaped the box. Encapsulated in this simple demonstration are some fundamental implications. The findings suggest that babies may well be attuned to different kinds of expectancies for events which are fundamentally built on a concept of probabilities. Another crucial implication is that this is a pre-linguistic ability. In addition, other studies, not based on the preferential looking procedures, by Girotto and colleagues show that older children follow probabilistic principles (including Bayesian ones) in their explicit probabilistic reasoning. They show that while preschoolers are not able to make correct numerical evaluations they are able to judge correctly which of two events is more likely to occur.

All in all, at least for probabilistic reasoning, the concepts may be so profoundly necessary that they are inbuilt, or the mechanisms that enable the sensitivity to processing them are learnt before language. It may be that Piaget's claims about child development were biased by the general deification of logical reasoning. Rather than a developmental track moving towards logical operations that takes us from childhood into adulthood via language, Girotto's work suggests that we already possess core reasoning abilities that take shape as we develop, they just happen to be probabilistic concepts.

Looking into the crystal ball: a personal reflection on the future of research on reasoning

This book was designed to do many things. For a start it was designed to be a forum that could bring together work from different avenues of reasoning research. In this way the reader can get a sense of the current research interests and the empirical techniques that are used to examine reasoning. The second motivation for this book was to give authors the opportunity to speak freely and speculate about theoretical ideas and interpretations of their findings, as well as making bold claims about the implications of their work for our understanding of reasoning. The third motivation is one that we cannot yet gauge, and that is to inspire new interest in young researchers by presenting them with questions and issues that are important and that will potentially lead to the next wave of research trends in the study of reasoning.

Given the potted history of reasoning research I presented at the start of this chapter, and given the review of the current work that researchers are conducting, we can see that many recurring themes are likely to be of interest in the near distance future. For instance, regardless of whether we have two systems of reasoning, or eight, or just one, we mediate between different representations. This issue will still be of interest to researchers in the future. Whether the reasoning process can be ultimately explained by neuroscience, neurogenetics or behavioural psychology, we are still looking for answers as to what the process is that enables us to switch from one interpretation of a reasoning problem to another radically different interpretation. Is it a supervisory system that arbitrates between the various different ways of interpreting and reasoning about a problem, be it moral, probabilistic, statistical, causal or deductive? Is it an inhibitory mechanism? Is it the same mechanism that is found in other types of cognitive processes, such as cognitive control? We don't know, but I imagine that research will be focused on these issues for some time yet.

Long gone are the days where researchers relied solely on paper and pencil tasks. Reasoning research has moved on from this for quite a while now. But what this means is that the data we use to understanding reasoning processes is rich. We now have reaction times, looking times, brain scans, genetic material. Lest we forget, we have IQ score, working memory, thinking styles, verbal fluency, spatial ability, emotional reactivity and social dispositions which we can measure and bring into our understanding of how people reason. The co-ordination of these measures to bring about better insights into questions about how we reason, and how other cognitive processes and social processes are implicated, is still likely to be a major research theme. The point here also is that the tools of measurement have shifted from paper and pencil tasks to much more elaborate and richer methods, and we can now examine reasoning as a dynamic process. People make inferences, update the inferences from the evidence they get, people may revise what they infer, and then draw new inferences, and so it goes on. Historically, the approach taken to understanding this updating dynamic process was via Wason's 2-4-6 hypothesis testing task. But, we're a long way from that now. Just as we shifted away from deeming logic to be the answer to understanding reasoning, we are likely to shift to a different view of reasoning. With new tools of measurement comes a change in the conceptualization of the reasoning process.

For instance, causal learning and reasoning research has shown the traditional reasoning community a new way of examining this process through interactive experimental tasks. These tasks require people to implement their inferences via practical choices that involve making changes, in effect intervening to change an outcome. This blend of reasoning and decision-making perhaps reflects a typical combination of processes in the real world that hasn't quite attracted much interest until now. The success it has enjoyed, and will likely continue to enjoy for a while yet, is because there is a normative framework (Bayes-Nets, and Causal Bayes-Nets) that can be used to judge inferences against. While it makes some assumptions that researchers have shown don't quite reflect psychological casual reasoning, it appears to be a framework that the causal reasoning community has mostly agreed provides a way of modelling reasoning behaviour.

It is clear that cognitive modelling is a fashionable research line, and an important one, and it may well dominate future reasoning research. Cognitive modelling has been a feature sorely missing from mainstream research in reasoning, until now. The direction, perhaps one that many traditional reasoning researchers may not like, but will have to face, is that the demands for cognitive modelling are increasing, because of the way in which the cognitive science community is operating and because research on reasoning is expanding into other areas of cognitive research. We may get to answer a fundamental question as a result – *what is the basic unit of knowledge in reasoning?*While we have made advances in understanding the types of mechanisms that enable us to learn about combinations of events in the world, and the way in which we infer those relations, in the context of causal reasoning, there is still vast disagreement as to whether our knowledge of those relations reduces to causal structures, propositions (rules) or associations. If ever we wondered what the basic unit of knowledge is, then perhaps understanding how we reason about causes will tell us once and for all, if all our processes about relations between representations can be broken down to either causal structures, rules or association.

The social aspects of reasoning have been of relevance since the 80s when researchers showed that particular kinds of contexts revealed our ability to reason correctly as determined by various normative models. But the relevance of social factors goes beyond just this. We make inferences about the intentions of others, we infer the actions people have taken from the goals we assume they want to achieve. We make predictions in social contexts by some form of induction, and we evaluate and track multiple changing arguments within social dynamic interactions. Moreover, we make moral judgments and adapt and change them within social contexts. The trend in including social factors into research on reasoning has existed for some time. But, given the rise in interest in moral reasoning, and the work of social psychologists interested in reasoning, the combination of socio-moral reasoning is likely to attract further research interest.

This is wishful thinking, but the research theme that I would hope would find its way most in the future is understanding reasoning as a dynamic process, just as in the same way as learning, memory, perception, attention and decision-making are understood as dynamic processes. Now that the techniques are ready for us to use, and the models are there for us to implement, and the contexts in which we reason have already been established, the researchers of the future have all the tools, and perhaps the conceptual apparatus to begin to uncover the dynamics of the reasoning process.

References

Ball, L. J., Lucas, E. J., Miles, J. N. and Gale, A. G. (2003). Inspection times and the selection task: What do eye-movements reveal about relevance effects? *The Quarterly Journal of Experimental Psychology*, *56*, 1053–1077.

Blaisdell, A. P., Sawa, K., Leising, K. J. and Waldmann, M. R. (2006). Causal reasoning in rats. *Science*, *311*, 1020–1022.

Braine, M. D. (1978). On the relation between the natural logic of reasoning and standard logic. *Psychological Review, 85*, 1–21.

Bruner, J. S., Goodnow, J. J. and Austin, G. A. (1956). *A study of thinking*. New York: Wiley.

Chater, N. and Oaksford, M. (1999). Ten years of the rational analysis of cognition. *Trends in Cognitive Sciences, 3*, 57–65.

Cheng, P. W. and Holyoak, K. J. (1985). Pragmatic reasoning schemas. *Cognitive Psychology, 17*, 391–416.

Cheng, P. W., Holyoak, K. J., Nisbett, R. E. and Oliver, L. M. (1986). Pragmatic versus syntactic approaches to training deductive reasoning. *Cognitive Psychology, 18*, 293–328.

Cherniak, C. (1984). Prototypicality and deductive reasoning. *Journal of Verbal Learning and Verbal Behavior, 23*, 625–642.

Cofer, C. N. (1957). Reasoning as an associative process: III. The role of verbal responses in problem solving. *The Journal of General Psychology, 57*, 55–68.

Cohen, L. J. (1981). Can human irrationality be experimentally demonstrated? *Behavioral and Brain Sciences, 4*, 317–331.

Collis, K. F. (1971). A study of concrete and formal reasoning in school mathematics. *Australian Journal of Psychology, 23*, 289–296.

Cosmides, L. and Tooby, J. (1994). Beyond intuition and instinct blindness: Toward an evolutionarily rigorous cognitive science. *Cognition, 50*, 41–77.

De Neys, W. (2006). Dual processing in reasoning: Two systems but one reasoner. *Psychological Science, 17*, 428–433.

De Neys, W., Vartanian, O. and Goel, V. (2008). Smarter than we think: When our brains detect that we are biased. *Psychological Science, 19*, 483–489.

Dennett, D. C. and Kinsbourne, M. (1992). Time and the observer: The where and when of consciousness in the brain. *Behavioral and Brain Sciences, 15*, 183–247.

Deutsch, J. A. (1956). A theory of insight, reasoning and latent learning. *British Journal of Psychology, 47*, 115–125.

Dunbar, K. and Klahr, D. (1989). Developmental differences in scientific discovery. In D. Klahr and K. Kotovsky (Eds.), *Complex information processing: The impact of Herbert A. Simon* (pp. 109–143). Hillsdale, NJ: Erlbaum.

Ennis, R. H. (1976). An alternative to Piaget's conceptualization of logical competence. *Child Development*, 14, 903–919.

Ericsson, K. A. and Simon, H. A. (1980). Verbal reports as data. *Psychological Review, 87*, 215–251.

Ericsson, K. A. and Simon, H. A. (1985). *Protocol analysis*. Cambridge, MA: MIT Press.

Evans, J. S. B. T. (1984). Heuristic and analytic processes in reasoning. *British Journal of Psychology, 75*, 451–468.

Evans, J. S. B. T. (1996). Deciding before you think: Relevance and reasoning in the selection task. *British Journal of Psychology, 87*, 223–240.

Evans, J. S. B. T., Ball, L. J. and Brooks, P. G. (1987). Attentional bias and decision order in a reasoning task. *British Journal of Psychology, 78*, 385–394.

Evans, J. S. B. T. and Wason, P.C. (1976). Rationalization in a reasoning task. *British Journal of Psychology, 67*, 479–486.

Fugelsang, J. A. and Thompson, V. A. (2003). A dual-process model of belief and evidence interactions in causal reasoning. *Memory and Cognition, 31*, 800–815.

Galotti, K. M. (1989). Approaches to studying formal and everyday reasoning. *Psychological Bulletin, 105*, 331–351.

Gazzaniga, M. S. (2011). *Who's in charge? Free will and the science of the brain*. New York: Ecco.

Gentner, D. (1989). The mechanisms of analogical learning. In S. Vosniadou and A. Ortony (Eds) *Similarity and analogical reasoning*. Cambridge: Cambridge University Press.

Gigerenzer, G. and Hug, K. (1992). Domain-specific reasoning: Social contracts, cheating, and perspective change. *Cognition, 43*, 127–171.

Goel, V., Gold, B., Kapur, S. and Houle, S. (1997). The seats of reason? An imaging study of deductive and inductive reasoning. *NeuroReport, 8*, 1305–1310.

Griggs, R. A. and Cox, J. R. (1982). The elusive thematic-materials effect in Wason's selection task. *British Journal of Psychology, 73*, 407–420.

Haan, N., Weiss, R. and Johnson, V. (1982). The role of logic in moral reasoning and development. *Developmental Psychology, 18*, 245.

Haidt, J. (2001). The emotional dog and its rational tail: A social intuitionist approach to moral judgment. *Psychological Review, 108*, 814–834.

Hamlin, J. K., Wynn, K. and Bloom, P. (2007). Social evaluation by preverbal infants. *Nature, 450*, 557–559.

Henle, M. (1962). On the relation between logic and thinking. *Psychological Review, 69*, 366–378.

Holyoak, K. J. and Cheng, P. W. (1995). Pragmatic reasoning with a point of view. *Thinking and Reasoning, 1*, 289–313.

Hunt, E. B. (1962). *Concept learning: An information processing problem.* New York: Wiley.

Huttenlocher, J. (1968). Constructing spatial images: A strategy in reasoning. *Psychological Review, 75*, 550–560.

Johnson-Laird, P. N. (1975). Models of deduction. In R. J. Falmagne (Ed.), *Reasoning: representation and processing in children and adults*. Hillsdale, NJ: Erlbaum.

Johnson-Laird, P. N. (1999). Deductive reasoning. *Annual Review of Psychology, 50*, 109–135.

Johnson-Laird, P. N. and Steedman, M. (1978). The psychology of syllogisms. *Cognitive Psychology, 10*, 64–99.

Kagan, J., Pearson, L. and Welch, L. (1966). Conceptual impulsivity and inductive reasoning. *Child Development, 37*, 583–594.

Kahneman, K. (2011). *Thinking, fast and slow*. New York: Farrar, Straus and Giroux.

Kintsch, W. and Monk, D. (1972). Storage of complex information in memory: Some implications of the speed with which inferences can be made. *Journal of Experimental Psychology, 94*, 25–32.

Lawson, A. E. (1978). The development and validation of a classroom test of formal reasoning. *Journal of Research in Science Teaching, 15*, 11–24.

Leahey, T. H. (1980). A chronometric analysis of simple deductive reasoning. *The Journal of General Psychology, 102*, 225–232.

Levine, M. (1966) Hypothesis behaviour by humans during discrimination learning. *Journal of Experimental Psychology, 71*, 331–338.

Manktelow, K. I. and Evans, J. S. B. T. (1979). Facilitation of reasoning by realism: Effect or non-effect? *British Journal of Psychology, 70*, 477–488.

Marcus, S. L. and Rips, L. J. (1979). Conditional reasoning. *Journal of Verbal Learning and Verbal Behavior, 18*, 199–22.

McGonigle, B. and Chalmers, M. (1977) Are monkeys logical? *Nature, 267*, 694–697.

McGonigle, B. and Chalmers, M. (1992). Monkeys are rational! *The Quarterly Journal of Experimental Psychology, 45*, 189–228.

Mogar, M. (1960). Children's causal reasoning about natural phenomena. *Child Development, 31*, 59–65.

Nisbett, R. E., Krantz, D. H., Jepson, C. and Kunda, Z. (1983). The use of statistical heuristics in everyday inductive reasoning. *Psychological Review*, *90*, 339–363.

Nisbett, R. E. and Wilson, T. D. (1977). Telling more than we can know: Verbal reports on mental processes. *Psychological Review*, *84*, 231–259.

Oaksford, M. and Chater, N. (1994). A rational analysis of the selection task as optimal data selection. *Psychological Review*, *101*, 608–631.

O'Brien, D. P. and Overton, W. F. (1982). Conditional reasoning and the competence-performance issue: A developmental analysis of a training task. *Journal of Experimental Child Psychology*, *34*, 274–290.

Osherson, D.N. (1975). Logic and models of logical thinking. In R. J. Falmagne (Ed.), *Reasoning: Representation and processing in children and adults*. Hillsdale, NJ: Erlbaum.

Pezzoli, J. A. and Frase, L. T. (1968). Mediated facilitation of syllogistic reasoning. *Journal of Experimental Psychology*, *78*, 228–232.

Piaget, J. (1952). *The origins of intelligence in children*. New York: International Universities Press.

Popper, K. R. (1952). The nature of philosophical problems and their roots in science. *British Journal for the Philosophy of Science*, 124–156.

Read, D. E. (1981). Solving deductive-reasoning problems after unilateral temporal lobectomy. *Brain and Language*, *12*, 116–127.

Rips, L. J. (1999). Deductive reasoning. *The MIT encyclopedia of the cognitive sciences*. Cambridge, MA: MIT Press.

Roberge, J. J. (1970). The effect of reversal of premises on children's deductive reasoning ability. *The Journal of Psychology*, *75*, 53–58.

Sloman, S. A. (1996). The empirical case for two systems of reasoning. *Psychological Bulletin*, *119*, 3–22.

Sloman, S. A. and Rips, L. J. (1998). Similarity as an explanatory construct. *Cognition*, *65*, 87–101.

Spelke, E. (1994). Initial knowledge: Six suggestions. *Cognition*, *50*, 431–445.

Sperber, D., Cara, F. and Girotto, V. (1995). Relevance theory explains the selection task. *Cognition*, *57*, 31–95.

Stenning, K. and van Lambalgen, M. (2008). *Human reasoning and cognitive science*. Cambridge, MA: MIT Press.

Sternberg, R. J. (1977), *Intelligence, information processing and analogical reasoning*, Hillsdale, NJ: Erlbaum.

Thaler, R. H. and Sunstein, C. R. (2008). *Nudge: Improving decisions about health, wealth, and happiness*. New Haven, CT: Yale University Press.

Trabasso, T., Secco, T. and Broek, P. V. D. (1984). Causal cohesion and story coherence. In H. Mandl, N. L. Stein and T. Trabasso (Eds.), *Learning and comprehension of text* (pp. 83–111). Hillsdale, NJ: Erlbaum.

Valett, R. E. (1963). A clinical profile for the Stanford-Binet. *Journal of School Psychology*, *2*, 49–54.

Vosniadou, S. and Ortony, A. (Eds.). (1989). *Similarity and analogical reasoning*. Cambridge: Cambridge University Press.

Wason, P.C. (1960). On the failure to eliminate hypotheses in a conceptual task. *Quarterly Journal of Experimental Psychology*, *12*, 129–140.

Wason, P.C. (1961). Response to affirmative and negative binary statements. *British Journal of Psychology*, *52*, 133–142.

Wason, P.C. (1966). Reasoning. In B. Foss (Ed.), *New horizons in psychology*, (p. 135–151). Harmondsworth, UK: Penguin.

Wason, P.C. (1968). Reasoning about a rule. *Quarterly Journal of Experimental Psychology, 20*, 273–281.

Wason, P.C. (1969). Regression in reasoning? *British Journal of Psychology, 60*, 471–480.

Wason, P.C. and Brooks, P. G. (1979). THOG: The anatomy of a problem. *Psychological Research, 41*, 79–90.

Wason, P.C. and Evans, J. St. BT (1975). Dual processes in reasoning. *Cognition, 3* (2), 141–154.

Wason, P.C. and Green, D. W. (1984). Reasoning and mental representation. *The Quarterly Journal of Experimental Psychology, 36*, 597–610.

Wason, P.C. and Johnson-Laird, P. N. (1972). *Psychology of reasoning: Structure and content* (Vol. 86). Cambridge, MA: Harvard University Press.

Wason, P.C. and Shapiro, D. (1971). Natural and contrived experience in a reasoning problem. *The Quarterly Journal of Experimental Psychology, 23*, 63–71.

Wharton, C. M. and Grafman, J. (1998). Deductive reasoning and the brain. *Trends in Cognitive Sciences, 2*, 54–59.

Woodworth, R. S. and Sells, S. B. (1935). An atmosphere effect in formal syllogistic reasoning. *Journal of Experimental Psychology, 18*, 451–460.

Wynn, K. (1992). Addition and subtraction by human infants. *Nature, 358*, 749–750.

Index